HOW TO MAKE A HABIT OF SUCCESS

by Bernard Haldane

WARNER BOOKS

A Warner Communications Company

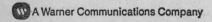

Contents

HOW TO MAKE A HABIT OF SUCCESS

Introduction

Just thirty years ago I counseled a man who was unsure of himself and earning $125 a week. As president of the nationally known company he joined then, he later employed another client of mine as his assistant—at today's equivalent of $40,000 yearly. These men, and many thousands of men and women like them, made this book possible.

I also thank an unnamed woman whose influence on a business associate brought me to the depths of despair in 1941—when I was fired. This experience led me to discover prayer, God, and the power of constructive faith. I learned "the hard way" myself, and I know I could never have done it on my own. I learned that each experience, including adverse ones when handled correctly, points a person toward greater success. The greatest power for success is love for one's fellow man, beginning with oneself; it helps provide the strength needed when difficulties—everyday roadblocks to progress—make the going tough.

* * *

Three presidents of the United States—Dwight D. Eisenhower, John F. Kennedy and Lyndon B. Johnson—as well as leading professional and management associations have commended the many applications and outcomes of techniques first described in these pages in 1960. A U.S. Department of Labor publication reports that the job finding system given in Chapters 9 and 10 is more than seven times as effective as generally available methods. More than that, the self-identification process (Chapters 3, 4, 5) has become basic to career planning programs in such leading institutions as Harvard and Columbia Universities, the Peace Corps, the Atomic Energy Commission, Exxon, Union Carbide, Smith-Kline and other corporations, and in all major religious denominations.

Japanese, Spanish and Portugese editions have been published, and digests have appeared in more than a dozen languages.

The Success Factor Analysis techniques given here have also been adapted in a variety of ways to help persons individually and in groups. These include the recovery and strengthening of self-confidence; upgrading of skills—especially those of women, minorities, youth and others who seem to face career limitations; military persons who must change careers or who seek second careers; factory, clerical and professional men and women whose jobs have become obsolescent; women who want working careers after fulfilling basic motherhood responsibilities; the great majority of persons who either do not know what they could do best, or who find their work increasingly frustrating. Success Factor Analysis has also been adapted to help college students identify the courses which are most likely to enlarge their potential for fulfillment.

Among the most satisfying applications to me is the use of these systems by many corporations to prevent lengthy unemployment of terminated employees, and by religious institutions to help clergy and laypersons leaving church jobs. Now personnel executives, guidance counselors, placement directors and faculty advisors—as well as peer group leaders—are being trained to use them in numerous institutions, colleges, high schools.

President Johnson said, "Private programs such as yours supplement the public effort to provide men and women with job alternatives and new futures."

In this time of increasingly rapid change, when persons entering the job market are likely to change jobs fifteen times during their working lives, I appreciate the public service being undertaken by Acropolis Books and its president, Al Hackl, in publishing this new edition. It will help many more thousands to know and use these techniques, and thus move towards greater fulfillment in their working lives. January 7, 1975.

Bernard Haldane

Bernard Haldane

Prologue

If you really want to make a habit of success, stop trying to learn from your mistakes. That's the first step!

People do not learn from their mistakes. I have learned that from my research and consultations with over 40,000 men and women over a period of more than thirty years. I have learned, also, that each person has his own way to success and his own kind of success. Your path to greater progress will not be exactly the same as that used by anyone else, even though the principles of achieving success are the same. This book is about the principles, and the Success Factor Analysis techniques based on them.

You can use these principles to build success into your life. They have worked for teen-agers, as well as for retired executives. Age and education are not bars to greater success, nor is the limitation of whatever experience you may have. The basic limitation is your knowledge of your own values, and your willingness to accept the responsibilities of being at your best most of the time.

It was more than twenty years ago that I started my search for these principles. But even in my early teens I was interested in people being happy and enjoying work they could do well, so perhaps my search really started thirty-five years ago. However, since 1940 I have trained business executives, government officials, educators and clergymen in the use of these principles for themselves as well as for others. I have taught them to career-puzzled college students—from freshmen to those seeking their doctorates. At the Harvard Business School, these principles were incorporated in a manual recommended to its thousands of alumni. The Society for the Advancement of Management recommended their use to graduating students in over 200 institutions of higher learning throughout the nation. And the American Management Association reported on them to more than 30,000 executive-members in all industries. Every progressive company has started to use these S.F.A. techniques.

Most people restrict their own potentialities. Nearly all of us are taught—at home, in our schools, and in most of our religious institutions—certain attitudes that limit our progress. You can see and appreciate these attitudes by taking a trip with me to Wonderland, and listening to a conversation between Alice and the Mad Hatter.

ALICE: Where I come from, people study what they are NOT good at in order to be able to do what they ARE good at.

MAD HATTER: We only go around in circles here in Wonderland; but we always end up where we started. Would you mind explaining yourself?

ALICE: Well, grown-ups tell us to find out what we did wrong, and never to do it again.

MAD HATTER: That's odd! It seems to me that in order to find out about something, you have to study it. And when you study it, you should become better at it. Why should you want to become better at something, and then never do it again? But please continue.

ALICE: Nobody ever tells us to study the right things we do. We're only supposed to learn from the wrong things. But we are permitted to study

13

the right things OTHER people do. And sometimes we're even told to copy them.

MAD HATTER: That's cheating!

ALICE: You're quite right, Mr. Hatter. I do live in a
topsy-turvy world. It seems like I have to do
something wrong first, in order to learn from
that what not to do. And then, by not doing
what I'm not supposed to do, perhaps I'll be
right. But I'd rather be right the first time
wouldn't you?

chapter 1

OPEN YOUR LIFE TO SUCCESS

There certainly seems to be a lot to what Alice says in the prologue. Just the same, you were told to learn from your mistakes when you were a child, weren't you? I was. All of us were.

And we were not told to study the right things we did, our achievements and successes. To do that would have been immodest, we were told.

I've asked lots of people how they go about learning from their mistakes. They all say they do. But they seem to have difficulty explaining how they go about it, and what benefits they get from doing it.

Do Your Ever Make Mistakes?

Of course you make mistakes. All of us make mistakes. All of us wish we made fewer mistakes. And it seems as though we all vow never to make the same mistake a second time.

But let me give you a warning right now. The more time you give to studying your mistakes, the more likely you are to increase the number of mistakes you make.

I won't say it's impossible to learn from your mistakes. But it comes very close to that. One obvious reason is that you are not really willing to study your mistakes; they are painful to think about, and perhaps embarrassing. The more you think about them, the more pain you inflict upon yourself. So it is reasonable that you stop thinking about them before you can study them thoroughly.

I'll say it again. People don't learn from their mistakes. When you admit your mistakes, as we are generally taught to do, you are following an ancient and charming practice which was invented to prove modesty and willingness to learn. Over the centuries, this quaint custom has been distorted, twisted to almost the reverse in meaning: "you can learn from your mistakes" instead of the old idea— "admit your mistakes and thereby indicate your willingness to learn."

The idea that you can learn from your mistakes is one of the biggest causes of failure, and certainly a stumbling block in the way of your increased success.

Everyone says you should profit from your mistakes. I have said it too. But if you do learn or profit from your mistakes, you should want to make more mistakes in order to profit more.

That sounds like nonsense, the idea that the more mistakes you make, the more you can profit. But it certainly follows from the idea that you can learn or profit from your mistakes.

Frankly, I am trying to shock you into realizing that something you have taken almost for granted just doesn't make sense at all.

If you are going to speed your progress, comfortably, you will need to break with some of the old practices which have been holding you back.

Every great advance by man has followed a break with tradition. Tradition and precedent must give way to principle. New principles, and old principles better understood, are the gateway to progress.

Tradition and precedent are, too often, crutches that support decayed practices.

For example, here's an outworn idea: "The burnt child fears the fire." There is some truth to it. But if a little girl who burned her fingers on a hot stove were to stay away from stoves forever, how would she learn to cook? And, again, how about those who played with fire, were burned, and then went on to found the Bronze Age, the Steel Age, and now the Nuclear Age?

Another example, this one leading to the point I wish to make: "If man were meant to fly, he would have been born with wings." Millions of people cling to that old belief, even though the 3000 mile Atlantic Ocean has shrunk to five hours of flight. The curious facts here involve the limitations of winged life as well as the accomplishments of man-made "wings."

The creatures born to fly are remarkably limited in their conquest of the air. Bees constantly overshoot their landings on blossoms. Migrating birds injure themselves by the thousands, flying into cliffs, tall buildings, trees and other obstructions. Soaring birds cannot venture into tumultous winds. And even radar-equipped bats are vulnerable to changes of light and temperature. Envious man studied their strengths and weaknesses for centuries, gave too much consideration to the latter, and wound up fearing their limitations.

During the last fifty years, man has taken a different scientific approach: he has paid attention to their strengths, added up their achievements alone. To these, he added some accomplishments of his own. Only then, by piling selected elements of one achievement on another, did man succeed in conquering the sky. Flight, radar and under-the-water sonic developments—these and other advances come not from brain-limited birds and fishes, but from man's observation of the uniquely effective uses they make of their "equipment."

Opportunity Unlimited

Some of the same rules that help man achieve scientific success also help corporations to make a habit of success. For instance, corporations study the relative profitability of their products. Profits permit corporations to grow, in much the same way as accomplishments and successes challenge a man to grow. Corporations are concerned with continued growth and continued profits.

The companies that grow most, the giants, have made a habit of success. Did they do it by concentrating on their least profitable products? Not on your life! They did it by concentrating on the products actually or potentially producing most profit. "Radio Corporation of America is progressing so rapidly that 80 per cent of its more than a billion dollar business is in products that did not exist fourteen years ago." The company said just that in its recent brochure on our current decade.

RCA dropped its outmoded and unprofitable products. RCA focused on using and developing products which have consistently carried it forward.

What does this mean to you and your success? It means that your opportunities can be limitless, if you will concentrate on applying your best and most profitable qualities or capabilities. It also means that you may be limiting yourself when you try to strengthen your weaknesses, or concentrate on avoiding mistakes.

Let's see what you would do in a situation like this. You know two very different men. One of them seems to fail at whatever he attempts. The other does better than expected with virtually everything he undertakes. Here you are, concerned with making a habit of success. Who's experiences should you study to benefit most: the repeated failure, or the constant success? Who's secret would you rather know?

Every successful man likes to have successful people around him. This seems to establish a "climate" in which success grows most comfortably. Consequently, since you

18

are planning to be more successful, you will want to study the experiences of the successful man, rather than those of the failure.

In other words, you should feel you will benefit most by knowing the "secret" of the successful man. His experiences are what you should study; and, as Alice said, you might try to copy some of them.

But has it occurred to you that you are both of these men: you have experienced both failures and successes. Yet it has been your practice to "let well-enough (your successes) alone." If you do unto others as you would be done by, you really should study your own most profitable experiences, your achievements and successes (not your mistakes or failures). If corporations can increase their profits by identifying their greatest "pay-off" items, you may be able to do it, too.

It isn't as simple as that, unfortunately. Until now, there has been no formalized method for the study of man's achievements.

What do I mean by "achievement?" What do I mean by "success?" It is likely that you feel you have no "great" or "earthshaking" accomplishments. And you haven't made your million dollars. I haven't made mine, either. So I had to meet the problem of defining achievement in such a way as to be understood and appreciated by each reader in his or her own individual way.

AN ACHIEVEMENT is an experience which gives you this combination of feelings: you feel you have done something well (what others may think of it doesn't count); you have enjoyed doing it; you are proud of what you have done.

A "success" is a high-quality achievement.

By these definitions, you have had "achievements" as an infant, in and out of school, in connection with many different segments of your life as adult, youth, child. It is the way you yourself feel about them that counts. An achievement is certainly something personal, perhaps something private.

It is not easy to think about or study your achieve-

19

ments. People who do that are called braggarts, conceited, and worse.

So let's consider a man whose reputation proves he was a 99 per cent failure. After only a few years of primary schooling, he was given up by his teachers as hopeless. Eventually he became a railroad newsboy and candy butcher on the Grand Trunk Line running out of Detroit, after which he "sort of disappeared" into a limbo of failure. In his late teens, he emerged again as a railroad telegrapher and tinkerer. For every thousand tinkering experiments he conducted, 999 failed. Not once did he look back at his mistakes, hoping his unseeing feet would carry him forward. "That's one more experiment I won't have to try," he enthused after a particular dismal flop. And by concentrating on only the most promising leads his experiments furnished from time to time, along about Experiment 5,000 Thomas Alva Edison produced the incandescent electric lamp.

Even as a child young Tom was interested in electricity. His inventiveness showed up early, too; it took the form of outwitting his father who insisted on interrupting experiments and making him go to bed.

Edison's biographies show him to be a man of purpose who was not concerned with mistakes and failures. He did not give time to dreaming up ways of how to avoid repeating his mistakes; his concern was always with achieving his objectives.

About Avoiding Mistakes

If you concern yourself with backing away from or avoiding repeated mistakes, you are not likely to find yourself "backing-up" into achievement or success.

It has been traditional to believe that the avoidance of mistakes will result in progress. Yet it should be clear that not getting what you don't want, is quite different from getting what you do want. (I believe Alice made that "clear.") For instance, the avoidance of war, is not at all the same as the achievement of peace.

Yet world-moving theories have been based on the idea that study of what is not wanted will somehow reveal how to gain what is wanted. Karl Marx developed one such theory. His monumental studies of the Industrial Revolution's ravages, its starvation, unemployment, slums, and great differences between the poor and wealthy— these led to his system to avoid inequities and hardships: socialism. Marx's thoughts were more about sharing the wealth, than about multiplying and distributing it. It took a capitalist concerned with multiplying and distributing goods, Henry Ford, to spark practices which have increased and spread wealth more evenly throughout the United States than Marx ever dreamed possible in his socialistic economy.

Be concerned with what you want, rather than with what you don't want!

Another world-moving theoretician gave his life to the study of the mentally sick. Dr. Sigmund Freud said that to be "normal" we must sublimate or redirect our natural aggressive feelings, and adjust with understanding to feelings of guilt arising from real or imagined mistakes (sins). Why should study of the mentally sick teach a man about normal behavior? Why should we learn to adjust to what is the worst in us, or what is wrong in our attitudes?

Instead, be concerned with adjusting to what is right and best in you. Learn about your best, and use this knowledge both to live up to your best and to overcome your difficulties.

Do you drive a car? If you don't, ask anyone who drives a car about this: What happens to the driver who concentrates on watching the ditches he wants to avoid, instead of keeping his eyes on the road he is traveling? The answer is, he ends up in a ditch.

If you want to avoid repeating your mistakes, and concentrate on how to avoid them, you are not likely to find success or make a habit of success. If you fix your mind on the problems and poverty you want to avoid, you'll end up with both of them. Job said it better: "That which I feared most has come upon me." On the other side, the man who led America from the depths of the de-

21

pression, "The only thing we have to fear is fear itself."

Be concerned with what you want, not with what you don't want! Let precedent give way to principle in your life. Recognise that happiness, achievement and growth are normal, and look for ways to increase them, have more of them. Of course sorrow, mistakes, sickness, rut jobs and problems are also parts of life; but the more attention you give them, the more you encourage them to settle into your everyday affairs. Attention is a kind of reward; and whatever you reward in life, you encourage to come back for more reward. Pay attention to the experiences which pay off most. Stop studying your mistakes; start and concentrate on studying your achievements and successes, however small they may be.

An important difficulty arises here. Suppose you have failed at something, or not done well at it; won't other people hold that against you? They probably will, but there are ways, described later in this book, to surmount obstacles like that.

It is so customary to look for what's wrong with people, rather than for what's right about them. "If you can't make good at one thing," says tradition, "how can you expect to make good at something else, something bigger?" But let's say you are a good quarterback, and the coach puts you in at tackle. You play your heart out, and get slaughtered. That still doesn't mean you are not a good quarterback, and might have won the game playing in your right position.

If you're put into the wrong job because of a company's "convenience," and turn in a poor record, it will be held against you. But you're less likely to get over that hurdle if you try to say how wrong the company is, than if you develop proof of how much more effective you can be for the company in another spot. The one way "blames" circumstances; the other takes control over your own progress—to the benefit of both you and the company.

Again, this requires that you become well-acquainted with your achievements, and the ingredients of those achievements. Throw modesty to the winds—false

22

modesty, that is. You'll admit to mistakes; so you might just as well admit to achievements and small or large successes. And you should consider this: the applause accorded the man who admits his failures is rarely so excessive as to include promotions to bigger jobs where he can courageously admit to greater failures. Besides, if you don't look at your achievements, why should anyone else?

We do have boasters and braggarts to spare, and they still dwell loudly on past "accomplishments." The big difference here is that you are not going to DWELL on past achievements; you are going to USE them and build on them.

In your pathway to greater success, you cannot USE failure, that is clear.

False modesty influences you to concentrate on your mistakes. It is only when you achieve, that you can express humility. "Let your light shine" it says in the Sermon on the Mount, "so that others may see your good works."

Who's Road to Success?

I couldn't estimate the number of qualified persons who have pointed out the road to success, and it would appear from the diversity of their directions that there are as many roads as there are advisers. There are indeed, just as many kinds of successes to be reached by them; but are they the roads for you, leading to where you want to go? And how do you know you'll like it when you get there?

There is a serious danger in following these "established" roads to success. Many of them are as out-moded as the directions for following the Oregon Trail. Many of them lead to goals that no longer exist, or are overcrowded, like the quaint ocean resort of two years ago that is now a mess of fishing piers, bowling alleys and dance halls. Today lives of great men all remind us that they made their lives sublime by altering the very circumstances that made them great. In his autobiography the great physicist Robert Millikan wrote: "For it has been the lot of all the generations of mankind up to the two generations my life span has covered to leave the world at death very much the same kind of place they found it at birth. But this will not be true of those of us who came from the vintage of '68. Our ordinary life experiences bear little resemblance to those of my father, and much less to those of my grandfather."

Most of our traditional rules of success have been passed down through so many generations that they are in a rut. What was good in one century was good in the next. No longer is this true. I'm not saying that the successful men of history would be failures in today's world. I'm thinking they would take one look at our existing opportunities, compare them with the meager few they had, and really take off. I'm also thinking they would find the rules for success they had used too restricting for modern living, and would use their rugged individualism to make a fresh start. Not for them the old recipe for rabbit stew: "First you catch the rabbit—" They would head for the frozen food department, and if their chortles in Sumerian, Egyptian, Greek, and Roman could be translated in general terms, they would add up to, "Boy, in this modern world how can you fail?"

The Break With Tradition

Every great advance by man has been the result of a break with tradition. If this were not so, we would still be savages, for man's intelligence today is no greater than that of the Sumerians of 5,000 years ago. According to Dr. George G. Hackman, Professor of Archaeology at Wagner College, the Sumerians had approximately the same Intelligence Quotient as modern man, but until they broke with tradition that had kept man roaming as nomads for generations, their intelligence had had little opportunity to manifest itself. When they settled down as city dwellers, one achievement had a chance to be related to another. They became clean-shaven, sophisticated

24

metropolites, with a culture in which all forms of art had time to flourish. So advanced did they become that in mathematics alone some of their formulas we now prefer to have handled by electronic computing machines.

The Sumerians did not fall through their lack of intelligence. They fell when they began to rest on their achievements instead of climbing on them. And once they began resting on their achievements instead of using them, the barbarians took them over with ease.

For century after century civilizations would rise laboriously, relax, and finally come to rest on their achievements. Then the "barbarians" would move in. So often was this same mistake made that we have a dangerous old saw to describe it: "History repeats itself."

Did we profit from the mistakes? The historians and military leaders from the Sumerians to the present made a great study of them, and they did do better. Each mistake, from the Sumerians' to World War II, has been bigger and more devastating than the last. But consider where we might be if each new civilization had been built on the achievements of its predecessor instead of on the rubble. Consider where we might be if we studied the successes instead of the mistakes. As a matter of fact, we have no choice but to study achievements. Any further study of mistakes leading to bigger and more devastating ones can only mean the end of the world. Thus the break with tradition becomes not only desirable but compulsory for both nations and individuals.

How This Applies to You

"Go ahead, make me a success," a retiring major challenged me. "That's all I want. I've been out of civilian life for fourteen years, and I've got a lot of catching up to do. Fast."

This happened soon after I was called in to found and direct a volunteer counseling and placement service for World War II veterans.

25

"Major," I said, "if you don't know where you are going, how will you know when you get there?"

"I'll figure that out when I arrive," he said.

But how could he? If you don't know where you are going, how can you know when you get there? If you don't know where you are going, there can be no recognition of your destination.

I'll leave the major there with his—and my—problem to take up my next client, a young lieutenant who has spent three years as an aerial navigator in the Air Transport Command. "I don't want any of the old stuff about roads to success" he told me bluntly. "Ben Franklin and Horatio Alger and the rest of those guys wrote all about it. Look, when I'm navigating a plane, I've got the stars, radio, Loran, Shoran, and radar to help me get where I want to go. I don't have to follow Columbus. I go where I want to go, and I've got all these aids to help me find the way. Don't you career men have some modern aids to help people go where they want to go? Or do we have to follow the same old roads as Ben Franklin's Poor Richard and Alger's newsboys?"

He was both bitter and right. Here was a young man who was not asking for the road to success. He was asking me for some modern aids that would permit him to steer his own course. He wanted to find his own success, and he didn't care if there was a well-marked highway leading to it or not.

I did have some aids to help him—signposts in his own past achievements that would permit him to set a confident course for his future.

Now there are dependable aids that will permit an individual to determine his own course and then help him get there. Starting in 1945 when returning veterans first made the question urgent, I have been able through my consultant work with corporations, military, government, and academic institutions, to amass well over 10,000 case histories based on interviews with over 40,000 men and women.

Since then, too, through my work in the executive counseling firm I founded, and through my work as career development specialist at Wagner College and Fairleigh Dickinson University, I have been able to confirm my findings so repeatedly, that I can no longer hesitate in setting them down. If they make obsolete some of the time-honored roads to success, so do they eliminate a lot of ruts. And instead of pointing out a road to a success you might not like when you get there, they help you select your own goal, and then, roads or no roads, provide the aids that get you there.

Your New Aids to Success

In recent years a great deal of importance has been placed on intelligence and aptitude tests. The military services use them. Industry uses them. Colleges frequently use them to determine the courses students should take. Maybe you have taken such tests and produced miserable scores and a resulting feeling of inferiority. Maybe you passed such tests with flying colors and still managed to end up at the bottom of the payroll. Whatever the result, the best thing to do is to forget it.

In 1954, social scientists headed by Columbia University Professors Thorndike and Hagen conducted a massive study of psychological aptitude tests. Nineteen different tests had been given to 500,000 men twelve years earlier. Seventeen thousand of these were studied. The study proved that the "scientific" forecasts based on these standard tests were not as good as guesswork. "Aptitude Test Is Found False Prophet On Jobs," headlined the N. Y. *Herald Tribune*. "They cannot predict success or satisfaction in your job," said Earl Ubell, Science Editor.

With your whole future at stake, it would seem then that the results of aptitude and intelligence tests—which are unreliable to begin with, and can be influenced by a good night's sleep, outside reading, a cold in the head or a hangover—are hardly conclusive.

But let's look at a future based on your past achievements. The achievements of weeks ago, or months ago, or years ago are not going to be influenced by the tensions preceding a critical examination. These are things you did well in the past, enjoyed doing, and which gave you a feeling of pride. Having done them once with gratifying results in the past, you can do them again, and kindred jobs in the future with equally gratifying results. Now we are not dealing with aptitudes hinted at in the course of a tense examination. We are dealing with demonstrated achievements.

Each achievement has focused and applied many of your best capabilities and other qualities. Many achievements, some small but all important to you, represent many occasions when your best capabilities and other qualities have been applied. Study of these achievements, then, will help to clarify their principal common "ingredients." These are your very personal qualifications. They point the way to opportunities and success in your own future.

chapter 2

LIFTING THE LID ON SUCCESS

The Capacity Myth

Recently I was asked to demonstrate and discuss Success Factor Analysis (the techniques presented in these pages) at the American Management Association—before a group of executives representing corporations throughout the country. They gave me the topic: "How to discover your capacity." I believe in man's unlimited potential, so I accepted the invitation as an opportunity to attack a long-established myth.

The conference chairman, who was aware of my views, indicated to those present that I was expected to produce a formula which would enable each of them to rate their capacities as though they were so many different-sized motors to be rated on horsepower. My opening remark was, "I will not talk on the topic of any man's capacity. This word 'capacity' indicates there is just so much a man can do.

"Capacity is a word that can't be applied to any man

of ambition. We can say a truck is loaded to capacity, that a motor is running at capacity, or that a theater is filled to capacity because we know their limits. Our scientists and engineers rate everything from the atom to the world's largest power plant in terms of capacity, but who is to say when our scientists and engineers have reached capacity and can 'hold' no more? Yet because this is a scientific age, with 'scientific' psychological tests—intelligence, personality and aptitude tests—we think we can measure men as we can measure a machine or a chemical reaction. We can't."

I paused to let that sink in, and then continued: "No inanimate object can be suddenly inspired to double capacity. Man does it all the time. Call it inspiration or determination, the fact remains that when a man concentrates on doing his best, he is constantly improving himself, his performance, and his over-all effectiveness. And as long as he is improving, how can he reach capacity? The whole idea is absurd."

"What I believe you really want to know is, how to determine the pattern of improvement of a man's best capacities." That evening, those successful executives learned how men are motivated—self-motivated; how men can be helped to know themselves—their best selves; how men can gain the self-appreciation which stimulates them to be and do their best more often. They learned what this book will help you to learn.

You need to know yourself, to be your constantly-improving best. And you also need to decide if you want to be your "best," or if you want to improve only your "average performance." There's a lot of difference between the two. If you want to improve "average performance," all you need do is cut down on mistakes—the safe and traditional way; but it must be obvious that the reduction of mistakes has nothing to do with the improvement of your best work. The reduction-of-mistakes approach merely raises slightly the level of mediocrity. Besides, if all you want to be is upper-crust mediocre, this book is not for you. This book is for men and women who are willing to accept the responsibility of individual excellence, for people who really want to be their best more of the time.

You need to understand what your "best" is; so you need to explore and appreciate those experiences which applied your "best" capabilities. *You* need to appreciate them. My understanding of what I think is your "best," will surely be different from how *you* feel about your own experiences. Only you know how you feel about your experiences. You may have done something that brought you praise and an increase in salary, but if in your own considered opinion it was a stroke of luck, that's all it was. Or maybe you worked to all hours completing a project that was greeted with apathy or even antipathy; it still is a big achievement if that is the way you feel about it.

One afternoon I was sitting next to the president of a professional organization at its monthly luncheon. As is my habit I prompted him into telling me of his achievements, achievements being my abiding interest. He listed a touchdown he had made at college, his election as senior class president, the first big contract he had landed by himself, and his election to his present post. At that point his friend and close business associate seated at my other side leaned over to suggest, "Tell Mr. Haldane about the boat you built in your basement. That certainly was an achievement."

"No," replied the president immediately, "that was just a little boat, a hobby."

Obviously the president considered as achievements only the successes that contained public recognition as an important factor. Another man building the same kind of boat might regard it as a masterpiece, a magnificent achievement in craftsmanship, project planning, and perseverance.

This is an important point. To create your own success and make a habit of it, consider only those achievements of yours that are important to you, regardless of what tradition, or your boss, or your friends might have to say about them.

The Nine-Dots Puzzle

We have one more obstacle to overcome before we can start building on your achievements. That is the boxed-in feeling. The feeling that a lid has been nailed down on one's opportunities to grow. By far it is the most mentioned obstacle of those who come to me for assistance, closely followed only by the question, "But what *can* I do successfully?" One has held the same job for seven years, and can't expect a promotion until his amazingly youthful and healthy superior dies or retires. Another is boxed in by six rivals in his department, all so evenly matched that the last time a promotion came up his boss hired a man from outside rather than break up an efficient combination. A third finds his capacity for growth restricted by the slow-but-sure growth of a century-old firm that prides itself on the number of watches it hands out every year to those that have served 25 years, usually in the same department. So, in scores of variations, runs the boxed-in theme.

Some years ago I discovered a revealing test that exposes the boxed-in feeling for what it is. It has opened the eyes of so many that I have every reason to believe that—unless you are the one out of a thousand that can solve it—it will help you, too.

In the space below are three sets of nine dots, thusly:

```
.1 .2 .3          . . .          . . .
.4 .5 .6          . . .          . . .
.7 .8 .9          . . .          . . .
```

The test calls for you to join all nine dots with four straight lines without taking your pencil from the paper. You have three chances, and I urge you to try all three of them, taking all the time you need, before reading further.

If you are like the 999 out of a thousand of the thousands who have tried it, you have spent some 15 minutes on the problem to produce nothing but frustration. You have been boxed in.

Now let's see what happened. In the first place, I introduced the test by presenting the enormous odds against your being able to solve it. And when you believe the odds are overwhelmingly against you, you will not try as hard as when you believe you have a 50-50 chance.

This is a dangerous policy, based upon what I call "statistical hypnosis." In this state you find it easy to believe that as long as thousands of others have failed, you are in good company when you join them. You are using statistics to lull yourself when, with a little individual resourcefulness, you might have found the problem made to order for you. To arouse yourself from this state, you need but remember you are not a statistical unit to be told that you will fail because thousands of others did. You are unique. What applies to thousands does not necessarily apply to you. Sometime early in 1960 a child was born who brought the population of the United States to 180,000,000. He became the last zero on a string of seven, according to statistics, but I doubt he will think of himself as zero reduced to the seventh power. Of this, too, I will have more to say later.

In the second place we have been taught so many things that restrict or limit our achievement potential that even in our contemplation of the nine dots we tend to restrict our imaginations instead of turning them loose. Since infancy we have been trained to conform, whether it be with playmates, fellow-students, or fellow-workers. In some instances these efforts to conform—to keep up with the crowd—have led to enormous bursts of energy and productivity. Oddly enough, however, most of these bursts of energy were spent, not on getting ahead, but on trying to bring one's lesser attributes up to par, or trying to cut one's superior talents down to par. Today, except in a few enlightened schools, the fate of the gifted child is a lonesome one.

To confuse matters, in certain activities like athletics, dramatics, art, and craftsmanship, an undue stress is placed on excellence. The boy who scores a touchdown at a critical moment is not hailed as a good player but as a football "hero." The girl who sings the lead in the school opera is not just a competent singer but the "star." By the same token, the boy who fumbles the ball and loses the game can crash from "hero" to "bum" in one five-second play. The boy in shop who gouges a piece of woodwork, though he be the best chemist in his class, has revealed himself as a "clumsy dolt." Scars like that can be of long duration, and even permanent. I know of an actor whose career was nearly ruined in college by the mistake of the leading lady in a dramatic club play. At the high point of the melodrama, with the heroine gazing expectantly at the wrong door, he made his entrance at the opposite side of the stage. Deadly silence, followed by a roar of laughter that broke up the play. It was the girl's mistake, but it was his entrance, and he became the goat. "They laughed at me everytime they saw me on the campus after that," he told me miserably. "Why, the next fall, in my first day in class, the professor greeted me with, 'Well, Lawrence, I'm glad to see you managed to find the right door.'"

I was a long time in working with him before he convinced himself that his real achievements in acting had not been ruined by another party's mistake. He returned to the stage and television where he is now enjoying increasing success. Not all are so fortunate. Achievements tend to be minimized; mistakes tend to be amplified, even though they be another's mistakes, and so strong has tradition made this influence that one girl's mistake had nearly caused him to abandon the career of his choice.

If that is true of the career fields based on visible activities like athletics and dramatics, consider how much more insidious it becomes in the intellectual, commercial, industrial, and governmental fields where success is not based necessarily on a starring role or a grandstand play. The evidence indicates that we attach much greater importance to the things we see, the visible careers, than we do to the intellectual—including memory—activities that are invisible. At the same time, not more than 50,000 people can be considered relatively successful in the fields

34

of dramatics, sports and arts. The rest of us 179,950,000 must find our successes elsewhere. But how are we to find them, if, for the most part, the fields are "invisible"?

That is tradition asking the question. In science, industry, and government an entirely new appreciation of these so-called invisible talents has been reached. These bodies know that ideas are the currency of progress. They know that not one wheel can turn until an idea stirs it, that not one board can be nailed to another unless an idea directs the motions, that no world peace can be reached until the ideas have been hatched to base it on. They know, too, that ideas without management skills to keep them organized, without craftsmen's skills to see them realized in finished form, and without operators' skills to make them work are just empty dreams. They need successful men in all these fields if they are to succeed themselves.

Tests

To that end they developed all sorts of tests. Their hope was that the future physicist, rampaging through a technical aptitude test battery, would stand out amongst his rivals as conspicuously as the football star rampaging off to his All-American title. In the same way they hoped to identify the future diplomat, the spaceman, the natural resources conservationist, the heart specialist, and the millions of others needed to be successful in some 30,000 varieties of jobs, changing at the rate of 4% yearly.

But it is one thing to test for the right man, and another to get the right man to take the test. All too often the job is handed to the one with the highest score, and in too many cases that score can be very low indeed. In those instances both the job and its winner suffer. These tests apply what I referred to earlier as the "capacity myth."

At this point I break not only with tradition but with modern practices, both of which are working backward. According to tradition, in analyzing the lives of great men,

35

we accept first their greatness, and then search through their pasts for the achievements that made them great. That is easy to do. With Edison we can say he invented the electric lamp, the phonograph, the motion picture, and more than a thousand other items. But what did Edison think about his inventions? Were they real achievements in his own mind, or were they only the by-products of some secret problem that, once conquered, led the way to all his other victories? And what about George Washington at Valley Forge? Did he think of that bitter winter as an achievement in heroic fortitude, as history has it, or did he think of it as a stupid trap into which he never should have fallen? Only the individual can know his own achievements, and only the individual can use them. Otherwise we would be what the Communists call "the masses" instead of a collection of 200,000,000 individuals.

Just as one cannot select certain achievements in the life of a great man and say, "These are what made him feel great," neither can available psychological tests determine who is going to become great in the future, and who is doomed to lasting failure. Only you can decide what you are going to become and the moment of decision is reached when you declare yourself open to success.

Now let's return to the nine-dot test. Did you box yourself in, or did you let your imagination roam beyond the limits of traditional confines? Here's the way it works: The first line is drawn through dots one, four, and seven. Tradition would have you stop there, but nothing in the rules prohibits you from continuing on down the page as long as the line is straight. Do so to an imaginary Dot ten, which will be, if your imagination is working right, in line with dots eight and six. Thus your second line will be from Dot ten through dots eight and six. Don't stop. By projecting your imagination, you will also project the line to an imaginary dot even with dots three, two, and one. That becomes your third straight line, after which your fourth can pass only through dots five and nine.

Simple, isn't it? And do not think I tricked you, or that it was, to use a current expression, a rigged show. If you really want to get ahead, you must be willing to work beyond what your eye can see. Increased success requires that you look beyond where you are to where you want to be. The visible confines must be lifted to provide room in which your imagination can rove. Your past achievements were not just a pattern of dots adding up to a box on which you pull the lid down on yourself. They contain the clues through which you get to know your best self and solve the problems of success by throwing off the lid on your ambitions.

More Aids to Success, and Where to Look for Them

"I yam what I yam," says Popeye, the famous comic strip character, "because that's what I yam."

A statement like that has been accepted for so many centuries that it has gained the stature of a truism. You are what you are, it would have you believe, and nothing can change you. But if that is the case, why do we worry about our young geniuses doomed to a life of mediocrity through lack of educational opportunities that would transform them into scientists and engineers? And why do we worry about the young Russians being developed into scientists when in back of them is nothing but centuries of serfdom? Change is inherent. Change is unavoidable. Merely because changes came slowly for a few million years doesn't mean they are still inching along today. Those first aeons were like the first few moments of a three-stage rocket taking off for space. A dreadfully slow, heart-stopping struggle to overcome inertia, a gradual pick up in speed, followed by acceleration such as only could be imagined fifteen years ago.

Here are some others that have received general acceptance: "Like father, like son," "A chip off the old block," or, by way of contradiction, "From shirt sleeves to shirt sleeves in three generations." Mark Twain was not like his father. Professor Millikan was not a chip off the old block. The Rockefeller brothers are not sweating it out as laborers in their shirt sleeves. When it comes to personal success, as a matter of fact, we don't have another old saw, "Exceptions prove the rule." Exceptions *are* the rule.

As I have pointed out, any change, any break with tradition, is as painful as running away from home. That is because our thinking is still based on training inherited from the past while our careers are linked to the swift pace of the future. Willy-nilly, ready or not, our scientists have tossed us into a changed world. What is more, while the scientists have been perfectly willing to do the tossing, they have been notably remiss in providing the nets in which to catch us. Having proved otherwise, they no longer believe that what goes up must come down. And since they have proved the point, we no longer have to believe it either. Neither do we have to believe that pride goeth before a fall, if pride is based on achievement.

I'm not going to get philosophical. I am a career development specialist, and as such I can recognize opportunities as they are created without having to create them myself. And they are being created at a fantastic rate. R. G. LeTourneau, who welds together the world's largest earth-moving equipment, says that had he been born ten years earlier, the best he could have achieved would have been a job as a blacksmith.

Or I could take my own field. A hundred years ago careers were not so much developed as thrust upon apprentices whether they liked them or not. The opportunities available were much the same as they had been for centuries. But as of the moment I am writing on an electric typewriter that is in itself the embodiment of thousands of new opportunities. As a business machine it is a part of the clan that range from vest pocket dictation machines to giant electronic computers. The plastic in its keys comes from a new world of petro-chemicals. Its nylon ribbon represents another world of synthetic fibers. The paper that receives the impression is the product of a lumbering industry revolutionized in the last generation. The ink, the metals, the glass-fiber insulation, and scores of other parts represent new products, or new versions of old ones, and hence new opportunities. And to think that a hundred years ago, I would have been sitting here writing on rough paper with a quill pen dipped in squid ink, and the only career suggestions I would have to offer would be the standard, "Work hard and save your money."

The very fact that opportunities are so numerous and so varied can in itself be confusing. A company executive may be aching to hire a man of your achievements, but in the meantime he must hire the best man he can get. A few exceptional personnel departments know the kinds of men their companies need, but that doesn't mean they always get the men they want. As a matter of fact, most executives are well-prepared to modify their pre-determined requirements of the kind of man they are seeking. Much as they might wish to reach out and grab a man with your achievements, that does you no good if you don't know what your talents are, where they can take you, and where to take them.

It was this impasse that attracted me to career work more than a quarter of a century ago. There was something very backward in a system that fitted inferior men into good jobs because they were "the best men available," while superior men fitted themselves into inferior jobs because they were "the best jobs available."

I couldn't blame the executives who did the hiring. In their quest for men of ideas and ambition, they were using the best aptitude and intelligence tests their personnel people and psychologists could provide. What they wanted was a net to bring in the good men, but what they devised was a protective screen that kept out both the exceptionally good and the least desirable ones. Yet at least they were trying, and if the right individuals did not come forward to be interviewed and tested, it was not their fault. By right individuals, of course, they meant right for the company. Should a highly superior man pass the tests for a job beneath his abilities, the hiring organization usually was not going to discard him for being too good. That was the traditional rule of business talking again—"Get the best you can for the money."

I am all for good bargains as long as they are in merchandise and not human lives. My own idea is that a job is not a hammer, a typewriter, a sales counter or a desk to be manned, though an organization may feel it should look at it that way. To me a job is the whole individual, complete with his intelligence, past achievements, and ambitions for the future. If the company hires the man for his skill with hammer and nails and then keeps him there—the job has to be filled—though he may demonstrate greater skills in another field, both man and company are losers. Hardest hurt is the man, with his one and only career at stake. He is jeopardizing his progress while his employer is getting what he pays for while losing the man's potential to produce more.

What it boiled down to is that while no employer would think of using a giant tractor to push a little wheelbarrow, he was all too often using human beings on tasks that left most of their abilities unused, while at the same time bemoaning the scarcity of good men. Well, that was tradition again, presenting its usual unreasonable logic. Tradition says the employer must get the utmost efficiency out of his machines, and the utmost efficiency out of the men on the jobs, and to that end all sorts of time studies and efficiency programs have been developed.

But if the man is not getting the most efficiency out of himself? That, says tradition, is his own look-out.

I looked over the advice provided by tradition to help a man look out for himself. "Grasp your opportunities," says tradition, about as helpfully as advising a drowning man to grasp straws. "Strike while the iron is hot," it says. "Break in," and "make good," and "get in the hay while the sun shines." It sounded like a lot of painful hard work to me, especially when my own idea of success was to be doing something you enjoyed doing well, to the mutual benefit of yourself and others.

In the library I found many books ready to help one achieve success. Inspirational books based on the lives of successful men who may or may not have been able to find their way around in our modern world. Books to restore self-confidence, books to send ambition soaring, books to keep you working through all of your hours of "spare time," books to renew your faith in the power of God. All were good books, and some were amazingly so. In fact, I found in them the encouragement to continue my research into what I came to recognize as their common weakness. They could help you if you knew where you were going, but no one of them could point out your way.

Having reached that point, I was brought face to face with a paradox: How to point out the way if the individual didn't know where he was going? I studied the psychological and aptitude tests that were assuming "voice of doom" proportions.

I could come to this conclusion. Psychological tests screen out, and do not screen in. The man who got the job too often was the last man "screened out," and there was no guarantee that he was the best man for the job, nor that he would like it when he got there. And the best of success books could only help the men who were already determined to get where they wanted to go, and hence were already half-way there.

At the same time, much though I might deplore men and women wasting their lives on jobs too small for them, I could see that the first move toward personal success had to be made by them. Even in enlightened industries—and the number is increasing daily—where special courses and training programs were being offered to those with the ambition to advance themselves, the move had to be made by the individual. So why didn't they make the move, even when being nudged in the right direction by their immediate superior?

When I reached that question, I knew I was getting warm. The best training programs offered by a company are the programs best for the company. In that respect I agree heartily with the companies. I want companies to become more successful through training programs that make their employees more successful when, as is fortunately often the case, the programs do as much for the individual as for the company. And that brought up a fine point. The companies spend thousands of dollars on their programs, they have made scientific studies of them, and they try to know how many trained employees for what jobs they will get out of them. But how much of a study had the employee made of himself to discover, if he could, whether the program would lead him to lasting satisfaction or merely a promotion to ultimate frustration?

That question has now been answered by the thousands of case histories of successful men in my files. The schools can educate you, and the psychological tests can try to rate you, and the training programs can try to train you. Opportunity may lead you one way, and a "lucky break" may suddenly lead you in another direction. This, tradition says, is the way it always has been and always will be. Man, it says, is the pawn of fate, and his best laid plans are no better than those of mice. These are all external influences, leaving you little to say, and tradition would keep it that way.

No longer is this necessary, if it ever was. From now on the guiding influence is going to come from within where it always should have been, and would have been if tradition hadn't taught you to profit from your mistakes instead of finding your successful self in your achievements. As I have said before, and will probably repeat at frequent intervals, only you can know your achievements, and in getting to know them you will meet, possibly for the first time, that most interesting and increasingly successful stranger who is yourself.

chapter 3

HOW TO FIND YOUR OWN GOLD

Where and How to Look for It

During the uninhibited days of the California gold rush, the only rule was that the gold was where you found it. The very term, "strike it rich," was indicative of the large part luck played in one's success. Of two men working the same creek within feet of each other, one could emerge a rich man and the other a pauper though both were applying the same amount of energy and talent to the job. And just to keep things interesting, lucky men are still finding gold in sizable amounts entirely by accident. Nevertheless, few are the modern mining companies that include luck as a major asset in the annual report to stockholders.

Today geology, minerology, and geo-physics are the sciences that have greatly reduced, though not entirely eliminated, the element of luck in our search for buried wealth. Aerial photographs reveal geological formations that the Forty-Niner couldn't suspect though he dug and picked his way over the terrain foot by foot. Electronic devices suspended below helicopters probe the earth like super-powered mine detectors, registering the presence of minerals far below the surface. Explosives are detonated to send shock waves into the earth, and sensitive devices record the echoing waves returned by different types of minerals and barren rock. When all of this data is patiently compiled, and then compared with the data supplied by mines of known productivity, the modern gold seeker has but to dig at the spot his scientific aids indicate as most likely.

The same principle is used by the modern navigator who uses gyro-compasses, radio compasses, Loran, Shoran, and radar to keep him safely on course through fogs that would leave helpless the navigator of only a few years ago. Man can see a port through solid fog, and make blind landings when, to use an airman's description, "even the birds are walking." He can see through solid rock, and find wealth the Forty-Niner wouldn't have recognized had he seen it on the surface. But what can he see of his own goal in life? And what does he know of the wealth contained in his own buried achievements?

Dr. Harlow Shapley, whose highly technical articles on astronomy have made him world famous, made this observation on humans during the long course of his observations of outer space: "Man has a deadly enemy at his throat, one that may succeed in returning the planet to the clams, kelp, and cockroaches. The enemy is, of course, himself. Man's worst foe is man."

What the celestial philosopher was driving at is that while man is perfectly willing to tackle the most dangerous forms of external exploration, from the explosive content of the invisible nucleus to the reaches of limitless space itself, he is extremely reluctant to face inward exploration. Wrote Dean Roy Pearson of the Andover Newton Theological School, "Whatever our fears of meeting other people, none is quite so great as our fear of meeting ourselves."

I am not going to discount the fact that this fear is

real. I have seen it too often. I have also seen its cause. Almost without exception, man fears to look back at what he was. The mistakes he made are still too painful. The first look at the past produces a wince, and a deeper look produces only a deeper cut. Instinctively, like the burnt child recoiling from the hot stove, he snaps his thoughts back to the endurable present, and assures himself that it is better to "let sleeping dogs lie."

That is like saying it is better to let the fog-bound ship crash, and the modern miner sink his pick in solid rock. It is the same old tired theory that a man profits from his mistakes. If one's past contains painful mistakes, it likewise contains rewarding achievements. If the Comstock Lode was one of the most richly rewarding strikes in history, Mount Davidson on which it is located is as big a pile of barren rock as one would care to contemplate. Hundreds of men dug into it and found *la borasca*—only the rock. But the Comstock is not famed for the thousands of failures. It is famed because from its wealth sprang railroads, and telegraph lines, and a substantial part of San Francisco. Who looked at a mountain of failure when the thin vein of success was what counted?

In the same way, why should you look into your past at the painful failures when it is your accomplishments that count? Merely because thousands of years teach that ships must crash in a fog doesn't make our modern navigators refuse scientific navigational aids. Merely because the search for gold was conducted for thousands of years on a hit-or-miss basis doesn't mean our modern gold-seeker must reject the scientific aids available today. And merely because the centuries teach that we must profit from our mistakes—a feat the centuries notably failed to accomplish—doesn't mean that you must work without the career development aids discovered in recent years.

No longer do you have to flounder around in a confusion of conflicting proverbs made authoritative only because they seem to have stood the test of time. Enough of those old sayings have been coined to fit almost any situation, but the same one that works for early birds is fatal for early worms, and hundreds of others can be equally treacherous when wrongly applied.

Not Where to Go, But How to Get There

Instead, we begin by looking into your past to become better acquainted with that unique, successful person who is yourself. This is by no means an easy task. If you are like most, you have been acting parts for so long, and adapting yourself to roles provided by changing circumstances that sometimes the roles become more real in your mind than your actual self. As Hitler's propaganda chief, Paul Goebbels, proved, a lie repeated often enough takes on the appearance of truth, and when that distortion takes place, conflict results. Not that you were lying when you adapted yourself to changing roles any more than the chameleon is lying when he changes color from place to place, but he may have some conflict in deciding what color he really is.

What we are looking for in your past are your achievements. That should be a pleasure, but immediately we encounter our old bugaboo, tradition. I know I have dwelt over-long on tradition, but you have no idea how much too long tradition has dwelt in you. A few phrases, no matter how often I repeat them, do not easily overcome beliefs so firmly planted by the centuries that they are akin to instinct. You may want to look for your achievements, but as I warned earlier, your first reaction is to shy away from anything that might make you look "conceited," or "too big for your britches." Forget it. Successful companies spend millions of dollars a year in advertising to proclaim the merits of their products, and what is good for companies is good for individuals when the claims are based on merit.

So let's get organized; an obvious suggestion leading to more complications. Recently I visited a friend who had become the chief adviser and organizer to the president of a $100,000,000 firm. On my previous visit I found him with a desk so neatly stacked with papers that the neatness itself was awesome. "I've got everything organized in order of importance," he had assured me. "In one second I can find any paper I need."

This time, not to my complete astonishment, I found him with a clear desk, while in his hands he held one manila folder. "You were right," he admitted wryly. "Those neat piles I was so proud of *were* distracting. As long as they were there, they reminded me of what I had to do, and I couldn't concentrate on the one job that was urgent. So I cleared everything off the desk except the job I was working on, and I've been able to concentrate like fury ever since."

He had discovered one of the basic laws of work: The more you have to do, the more important it becomes that you concentrate on one job at a time. Work organized for successful accomplishment is work organized to direct full attention upon the job in hand, with no dissipation of energy on nagging distractions. Yet it is not quite that easy. Before my friend could select the one job for his immediate attention, he had to concentrate first on some job planning. He had to familiarize himself with the values of all the papers before he could determine the order in which they were to be tackled one by one. Steeped in company policy as he was, the job-planning offered no great difficulty.

On the other hand, how do we concentrate on the over-all job-planning of a career when we don't know what course the career might take?

The traditional "rules for success" have no answer for that question. They would have you "set a goal," and "work hard" until you get there. The logic seems sound, and many determined men have achieved "success" that way, but just as often the results can be tragic. That distant goal selected at the age of 20 can turn out to be a dead end at 40, especially if the goal was one selected as the result of well-meant advice from parents, friends, teachers or employers. And then, tradition would have you believe, it is too late to start over.

Assay the Ore

By this time, you should have remembered and written down many of your achievements. If not, take the time to write down ten for a start. These might be relatively unimportant experiences to anyone but you yourself.

Like gold ore, your achievements have to be "panned" in order to find the nuggets, small and large. Your achievements have to be examined, and *la borrasca* separated from the gold. When you have the golden information, when you know your best self and your best capabilities, you will come to know the goals you want to reach. As each goal is gained, the habit of success becomes more deeply entrenched, and constantly bigger and more enticing goals become attainable.

Now to uncover your achievements. Of course I have asked that you make a list of at least ten, but if you have already done so you are an exception. If you are like most of us, you haven't been able to locate many, if any, significant achievements, mainly because they have been blanketed under layers of modesty. Or perhaps, like many of my clients, you have procrastinated in listing your achievements in the hope that I will reveal some magic words to make your success inevitable and spare you a lot of homework. I pause to shudder at where I might be if I possessed abracadabra of such potency. The fictional Svengali hypnotizing his little Trilby to singing triumphs would be a naive innocent compared to the man who holds the key to everyone's success.

Only you hold the key to your success, and only in your achievements is it to be found. So start writing, preferably in a new notebook that will in itself signify a fresh start toward success. Start with the first achievement that comes to mind—something you enjoyed doing, and did well, which made you feel good when it was done. But it must be written down.

Do not concern yourself with listing your achievements in chronological order, or in order of importance, or, least of all, with what others may have thought of them. Though we are all different, we all share many of the same talents, as the conformists are happy to point out, neglecting, however, to mention that no two individuals are equally strong in all the same talents, nor do they have the same opinions of them. And it is in these differences of strength and opinions that one individual differs from another. Sometimes we can see talents in some people showing up so strongly that we refer to them as born salesmen, or born actors, or born artists, and then we look at ourselves where these talents are conspicuous by their absence, and wonder if we were born with anything. For the most part, when we think of people born to this field or that, we are thinking of those whose talents were clearly evident quite early in life. I know a born sales manager who, at the age of nine, had four boys working for him on his paper route. My actor friend, so mortified at making a wrong entrance, declaimed to the cows in his father's barn when he was eight. General James Gavin had read all the military books in his local library before he was twelve, and Stanley Hiller of helicopter fame was caught speeding at the age of nine—in a scooter he powered with his mother's washing machine motor.

But what of those whose talents are not so conspicuous? Of those it was customary to say that their talents "showed up late in life," or that they "came as a surprise." Not so. Their talents were just as surely present early in life as those of their more conspicuous friends. What was lacking until recently was a means of recognizing them at all ages. Now we can not only recognize them, but we can apply them to fields of opportunity that didn't even exist when these talents were first demonstrated. I am reminded here of a four-year-old boy who plagued his uncle with questions like, "Why does a nail stick to a magnet?" and "Why does a compass point to the north?" and "What is magnetism, anyway?" In 1883 these questions indicated only that the boy was a nuisance, but at the age of 43 Albert Einstein won the Nobel prize for his development of the theory of relativity.

The age at which your achievements occurred is not important. However, in selecting your achievements—your veins of gold—be sure you include experiences that brought you personal satisfaction as well as accomplishment. That others might not have recognized them as achievements is of no consequence to you. For one achievement, such as winning a spelling bee, you might have received praise and a pat on the head. For another, such as collecting a dozen different eggs of song birds, you might have been soundly punished. For another, such as mowing the lawn for an aged cripple, you might have been rewarded with both cash and gratitude. For another, such as braving yourself to go off a ski jump, you might have been soundly punished. For another, self and the family bank account when the doctor bills came due. But no matter what your friends, parents, and neighbors might have to say about these incidents, the only thing that counts is your own opinion.

In an office across the street from me in New York sits an executive who "wasted" some 25 years of his life as a successful attorney in corporation and government work. When he first came to me, complaining of being frustrated in his career, I urged him to write down his achievements. "To get the best cross-section," I said, "list two achievements for each five-year period of your life. At forty-nine, you should be able to set down at least twenty."

He returned a week later with four. In high school he had completed the first album of what had now grown into a valuable stamp collection. In college he had set a record in selling more advertising space for the college humor magazine than any student had ever sold before. Then there was the day he celebrated passing his bar examinations. His fourth achievement was written in terse and bitter words: "The day I realized that after a quarter of a century on a sure salary, I wasn't getting anywhere."

He wasn't giving himself much to work on, but it was a start. The stamp album, for instance. He told me about it. His parents had objected to his hobby because it was confining, expensive, and a lot of nonsense adding up to nothing. They thought he should be out with the other fellows, spending his money on sodas, movies, and sports instead of stamps. His friends, or rather his classmates because he had no real friends, thought of him as a sissy, and certainly the girls found nothing of interest in a boy who could talk only of stamps. But in spite of the fact that the opinions of others condemned him to a lonesome childhood, he found in his stamp collection a release for his talents that he could find in no other way.

What talent, you might ask, as was asked then, is needed to paste a few stamps in an album? Very little talent, we can answer today, if only a few stamps were involved. Every child goes through a period of collecting a few frogs, turtles, snakes, coins, eggs, dolls, and countless other items, but if this acquisitive period is of brief duration, it is without lasting significance. The boy who collects a few butterflies is not necessarily a future lepidopterist, nor is the young coin collector destined for a place in high finance if a few coins are the extent of his collection. But when a hobby survives in the face of many obstacles, we can be sure it has the solid support of genuine talent.

Today we know that the genuine collector expresses through his collection a desire for ownership, a desire for independence, a desire to run his own business, or his own department, or conduct his own research. In real life he may work in a field far removed from that around which his collection is centered, like the jockey who collects paintings, or the financier who collects mushrooms, but when he is with his collection he is king. He has something unique, created by his talents, and his talents alone.

To return to my stamp-collector-turned-attorney, after 25 years as a corporation and government attorney, he still saw himself as the servant of others instead of the master of his own business. No longer was he looking upon his stamp collecting as a creative hobby but as a refuge in which he could escape the frustrations of daily life.

"Tell me what you have to do to be a good stamp collector," I suggested.

He didn't know. He hadn't thought about it. "I guess you just have to know the business," he said. Not much of an answer from one who had devoted much of his lifetime to his hobby.

"I think we've got a vein of gold here," I said, "and I don't mean in the cash value of the stamps you have collected. I know, for instance, that you have to be highly observant to be a stamp collector. You have to have a keen eye for color. You have to have an eye for detail that is practically microscopic. I know you stamp collectors can concentrate more intently on one square inch of stamp than can an art connoisseur on the Mona Lisa. You appreciate design. You are somewhat familiar with foreign countries. These are just the surface indications we all know about. As the expert in the field, you should be able to dig deeper. Suppose you write down a list of the talents you think a stamp collector needs, and why. While you're at it, you might as well write an explanation of how you were able to sell more advertising space for your college magazine than anyone else."

He did not find it easy to mine his own veins of gold, but no one has ever accused mining of any kind of being easy. We do have one big advantage, however, over the hard-luck miner. He must deal with matter, and no amount of mind-over-matter is going to bring two widely separated veins of ore together. But such is the human mind that we can combine two widely separated talents to produce a single vein of double richness. When several talents can be combined, the rewards can enrich all phases of your life, and mind truly has triumphed over matter.

In the case of my friend, he began by first recognizing that his stamp collection was no mere hobby but a release for a wide variety of talents. He found it harder to realize, after his years as a career lawyer, "taking the legal chores tossed my way," that his carefully nurtured collection was an expression of his deep, inner desire to be his own boss. Then, in analyzing his success as a space salesman for his college magazine, he found himself writing, "In the advertising department, I was what you might call the star. No one had to tell me where to go to solicit advertising." And as his own boss, he had set a record. No one was more astonished by this admission than he was. Like most people, he had never looked back at his achievement to determine some of its causes. Nor had he ever looked at it in terms of gold it might contain.

He had more difficulty in explaining why he considered passing his bar examination an achievement. Finally he wrote, "My parents had always wanted me to be a lawyer. I took pride in being able to please them." No one knows how many careers are ruined or handicapped when a dutiful child follows the dictates of his parents' ambitions instead of his own, but the number is horrendous. In this case, all was not lost. For all that my friend claimed to have been completely frustrated by his years as an attorney, a little deep self-examination revealed many accomplishments in which he could take pride. In the legal conflicts that crop up between men, and between corporations, and between governments, he had found great satisfaction in his ability to reconcile differences of opinion out of court. Under a little more self-examination, he was ready to admit that settling a case out of court involved a considerable amount of diplomacy along with abilities to arbitrate and negotiate, "but that sounds pretty conceited."

You see, he was still using the traditional word, "conceit," to slap down a realistic appraisal of his values. But at least he was beginning to feel "conceited" instead of "frustrated," and that indicated a healthy change of attitude. The next step was to combine these widely separated achievements into a single rich vein of ore. How he made that step will be revealed in the succeeding chapters, but by way of immediate encouragement, here is the result:

He is the head of his own department in charge of foreign and domestic sales. Through his artistic abilities and attention to details, he has been able to dress up his products, bring about improved performance, increase the effectiveness of advertising campaigns, and "build up the little fellow." Thanks to his legal training, the stringent laws governing international commerce that his competitors find so baffling offer him no difficulties. And his diplomatic ability to arbitrate and negotiate has kept his company on top in countries too often influenced by British, West German, Russian, or Japanese salesmen. He is mining all of his achievements to be a salesman of U. S. good will and his company's products. His one complaint:

"My wife and I are having so much fun on this job that I haven't been able to work on my stamp collection for months."

What I would like to make clear at this point is that the only advice he took in reaching his present position was his own. It is true that we had met at weekly intervals, but the only suggestions he needed were those offered you in these pages. I was the sounding board against which he bounced his own thoughts. The echoes returned to him, though amplified by my experience with thousands of others confronted by similar problems, were still his own words. Hence the reason for this book. These pages will provide a modern sounding board against which your own thinking will be reflected, and the words guiding you to success will be your own. In short, you will be like the modern navigator who sends out his radar signals, and reads the amplified echoes in his scope, or the modern miner who sends out his signals, and reads the amplified echoes in his detectors. The exciting difference here is that while the navigator is using his modern aid to probe space, and the miner to probe the earth, you will be probing for the right course to the rewarding ores within yourself.

The experience will seem a little strange at first, like the first time you heard a true recording of your voice, but don't let it bother you. Several of the best actors in Hollywood still squirm in anguish when they see rushes of their day's acting on the screen. Nevertheless, they persist, knowing that only through analyzing their best achievements can they continue to improve. For you, the next chapter will ease the way.

chapter 4

SOME CLUES TO YOUR ACHIEVEMENTS

You Can't Keep a Good Man Down—Or Can You?

When tradition says you can't keep a good man down, it is referring to a man who knows he is good, has confidence in his abilities, and has the courage to rise again. To that extent tradition and I are in agreement, but after that the break is sharp. There is something painful to me in visualizing a good man constantly climbing up after one defeat on top of another. I can admire his fortitude, but must deplore his career planning.

But rise he does, proving it can be done. To present another side of the picture that I have seen too often, a man doesn't have to know he's good in order to rise, if he just thinks he is. History is loaded with cases of "successful" men, including many a conqueror and business tycoon, who were no good at all but thought they were. Success under those circumstances seems merely a matter of attitude, so easily attainable it can be had for nothing more than an illusion. Unfortunately, success reached through an illusion is nothing but an illusion when reached, and no envy need be wasted on those who got "it" without having "it" inside to start with.

Those of us concerned with career planning cannot ignore the recoveries of good men who refuse to be kept down, nor can we overlook the often spectacular ascents of the pretenders. Both offer convincing proof that to rise, or make money, or achieve power, one must have as a chief ingredient a real or imagined confidence in one's self. By the same token, many a good man is down, and is being kept down, by lack of that ingredient.

To tell a good man he would do better if he had more confidence in himself is about as useless as telling an alcoholic he would feel better if he quit drinking. "All right, so I'm a good man," he is willing to admit, "but what am I good for?" And until he knows the answer to that question no amount of confidence is going to take him anywhere.

That's where past achievements come in. In coming to know them, and coming to know yourself, you come to know what you are good at. Once that is accomplished, you won't have to be told to have confidence in yourself. You'll already have it. What is more, because you will know how to base your success on your achievements, you won't be falling into the unplanned pitfalls from which the "good man" is constantly rising, his "head bloody but unbowed." Nor will you, like the pretenders, climb ruthlessly over others to reach what in the end is only a hollow victory. Real success is based on enjoying the challenges one meets in reaching a goal that brings mutual benefit to one's self and others, and that is what you will find.

There is sufficient evidence to prove that you were born with many of your talents, and some of them manifest themselves early in life. Most of these, as I have pointed out, are in the visible fields—the juvenile chess wizard, the child prodigy at the piano, the dancer who kicks to music in the crib, the kindergarten artist who paints realistic cows at five. But what about the rest of us who may have been born with talents of equal value, but which do not "show up" so early in life? Some valuable talents, in fact, are so inconspicuous that they remain unsuspected for years if detected at all. Other talents, though recognized, might be too expensive to develop, or too dangerous for childish tinkering. Ben Franklin flew a kite, and brought down electricity from the sky. Today we don't wonder that he produced an electric spark from his brass key. We marvel that he wasn't fried to a crisp. Today any father seeing his young electrical genius out playing with thunderbolts or trying to dismantle the family fuse box is more apt to wallop him than encourage his "suicidal tendencies."

There are some who condemn this attitude as overprotective, but they are not being realistic. Our grandfathers could operate on the theory that what a boy didn't know couldn't hurt him. Today the boy's opportunities for self-destruction—with the possible inclusion of his family and a few neighbors—are limitless, and so many of his most active talents are sternly smothered "for his own good." Piano playing—yes, but mixing up a batch of rocket fuel—even the government moved in to squelch that.

Nevertheless, these talents, though suppressed, continue to exist. Constantly they reveal themselves through your achievements, but most often they are so thoroughly disguised that only in recent years have they been recognized for what they are. For that reason every achievement that was the result of something you enjoyed doing and brought you satisfaction when accomplished should be listed. As of the moment you don't know what promises it might hold.

Let's consider the case of Albert Wilkins, 43, who came to me after ten years in a department store. His story is typical of thousands whose careers had been stunted at the start by the Great Depression.

"It was rough, Mr. Haldane," he said, "but no rougher on me than the rest of the fellows. We used to say that if a job lasted ten weeks, it was permanent. When I finally did get a job in a furniture factory that looked good for life, I was so grateful I didn't even mind hating the job. I'd still be there if I hadn't been drafted."

World War II caught up Albert and his depression-conditioned friends, and tossed them into four more years of chaos. They had job-security, but life-security was lacking. Four years of that, from North Africa to Berlin under fire most of the way and then, in 1946, Albert was turned loose with millions of other survivors in what was the biggest, most fantastic scramble for jobs in history.

"It was any port in a storm," said Albert. "I got a job in this department store as an extra during the 1946 spring sale. When they asked me to stay on as a regular after the sale at thirty-five a week, I could hardly believe my ears."

During the next ten years he had risen to become floor manager at $95 a week, so he could not be considered a failure. In his own mind, however, he was what he called a "successful flop." The storm that had blown him into the port had long since blown over, but he was still there, afraid to venture out. "I'm doing what the company wants me to do," he said. "Not what I want to do." Was it wise, he wondered, to change courses in mid-stream?

"Certainly," I assured him. "What course do you have in mind?"

He didn't know. Furthermore, faced with the fact that a change was possible, he wasn't sure he wanted to make it. Cold doubt began to replace hopeful ambition. His memories of his years of insecurity, when even his life was in jeopardy, suddenly conspired to make his present job and pension plan look very good after all.

"I guess I was dreaming," he said finally. "At my age I can't afford to start over. Not in competition with all the young fellows coming out of college."

A perfect illustration of a man boxing himself in. But at least he had dared dream for a while, which was encouraging. I had another reason for being interested. Only the week before one of my clients had enthusiastically reported finding his course to success in a department

59

store much like Albert's. This man, recently retired from the Army where he had achieved great success as a Post Exchange officer, claimed his new job was "exciting, stimulating, something new every minute." His buoyant enjoyment of his "new life" was as positive as Albert's resigned acceptance of his fate was negative. I knew from experience that it was now or probably never—there can be no irrevocable "never" placed on any man's career—with Albert.

I suggested that he tell me something about himself, things he enjoyed doing—and I am betraying no professional secrets when I say that is the best way to let the client hear some firsthand information about himself. (Oh, yes, I know about those who talk about themselves all the time, but those are the ones who lack the ability to listen.) The story came out hesitantly and in piecemeal, and that's fine, as long as it comes out. Reassembled in chronological order he revealed to me, and himself, that his grandfather had been a gunsmith and his father an expert tool maker. In the way of achievements he recalled that at the age of four, coached by his grandfather, he had taken apart a Springfield rifle, cleaned and oiled it, and put it together again. And, oh yes, at the age of ten his father had raised him to a dollar a week because he worked so hard in the basement metal-working shop his father ran as a side-line.

Nothing more? "No. When the depression hit, my father lost his job, I had to quit business school where I was studying accounting, and you know the rest. Anything I could get to help out, and not a good job in the lot. No achievements there. Just defeats."

And he was still defeating himself. He realized that as soon as I did and said defensively, "But I'll tell you one thing, I've got a metal working shop in my basement—my wife says I spend more on it than I do on the family—where I can make anything from a model locomotive to more machine tools for my shop—" and once off on that subject, he became a man transformed. This was no resigned floor manager before me now but a creative machinist who exulted in his work.

"But what good does that do me?" he asked, his original defeatist attitude descending again.

I suggested he do some more thinking on the subject, and return the following week with a list of more achievements. He returned with ten. Only ten achievements after 43 years of living, or should I say surviving. Included among them was the time during the war when he got a disabled tank back into action by machining a part himself, a system he had developed for keeping inventory records of the merchandise on his floor, and—the source of his last raise—the designing of some display racks that presented his merchandise to better advantage in less space. "Nothing to amount to shucks," he said.

Yet what a reservoir of unused talents those achievements revealed. Mechanical aptitude, a keen awareness of the flow of materials, an insistence upon clean efficiency, and an appreciation of the value of inventory records, to name but a few.

"Have you ever thought about combining these achievements?" I asked.

Albert lost a lot of confidence in me then. "They aren't even related," he said. "How can you combine them?"

"Maybe they weren't related when you were a boy," I said, "but they are now. Have you ever heard of production controls—the business of getting the right parts to the right machines at the right time to keep the assembly line going? It isn't even a job any more—it's an art."

"So what chance does a floor manager have in a job like that?" he asked, still boxing himself in, but brightening considerably.

"Not as a floor manager, no," I agreed. (I was not forgetting my ex-Post Exchange officer who had now risen to floor manager and was going great guns. The point is that the job that was for him was not for Albert.) "But as a man who knows machines, who can keep the materials flowing, and is a demon for efficiency—well, figure it out for yourself."

The details will be filled in later, when you learn more

about using your own achievements, but for the moment I'll assure you that Albert is the best production control manager, at twice his floor manager's salary, his machine-tool company has ever had.

In ranging through your achievements, sort of trying them on for size for the first time, you will find yourself saying, "Oh, no, not that one. I felt good about it at the time, but now I realize it was really pretty small stuff." When you do that, evaluating a previous experience in the light of what you know now, you are boxing yourself in. Each achievement must stand on its own in terms of what it meant to you at the time. This calls for re-creating the period in which the event took place, and then looking at it in as much detail as is possible through the eyes of the person that was you at the time.

When Albert Wilkins first mentioned as an achievement his machining of a part that restored a tank to action during World War II he was inclined to minimize it. It was a small part linking two treads together, and compared to the work he was doing now in his basement shop, it was crude to the point of being childish. Then he began living that day over again.

It began with a dawn, strafing attack, with the German planes coming in low over the hedgerows. One lucky shot through the treads, and a tank was crippled. In a demolished French garage he found an old engine lathe, but there was no electricity to power it. To turn the ancient belt-and-pulley system he had to recruit man-power, and then, jerkily, proceed to turn out the link. By the time he had relived that experience, smelling again the reek of the high explosives that had demolished the garage, and hearing again the blue language of the soldiers who blistered their hands turning his lathe, he could see that his achievement was not to be judged by the size of the part he had made, but its importance, and the resourcefulness he had used in getting it made.

In going through your achievements, don't hesitate to list those that are freshest in your memory, but don't stop there. Go back as far as memory permits. Einstein's interest in magnetism, which in turn led to his discovery of the theory of relativity, was revealed at the age of four. In like manner Indira Gandhi, the great political leader in India, lined up her dolls as a captive audience when she made her first speeches at the same tender age.

No period of your life should be neglected in your search for your achievements, nor should any one period be over-emphasized. When tradition says that the child is father of the man, it is stating a half-truth only. For centuries the boy who showed signs of becoming a good farmer—having little opportunity to show signs of becoming anything else—usually ended up as a good farmer, and so on through the other trades to which boys were apprenticed early in life. Then the boy was indeed the father of the man, and the belief was strong that a man's career was "settled for life" before he was 21. There was a saying to describe men who shifted about, hunting for something more congenial: "A jack-of-all-trades, and master of none."

The major break with that tradition arrived after World War I, announced by, of all things, a popular ditty that went: "How you gonna keep 'em down on the farm, after they've seen Paree?" Nor were farm boys the only ones influenced by that war. Men taken from all walks of life were exposed to influences they had never anticipated, and gone forever was the theory that the child had sired his own career and was stuck with it.

A theory had been seriously challenged for the first time, but nothing constructive had been offered to take its place. What of the child whose achievements promised to sire a highly successful career? For instance, one of my clients listed as his first achievement the fact that at seven he had stayed in the saddle of a run-away horse. No one can say how many children, confronted with a like emergency, clung to their saddles like leeches rather than take a header, but we can be sure most of them were more terrified than thrilled. This man, now a successful breeder of Arabian horses, could never get the enjoyment of that wild ride out of his mind. Always after that he had longed to be with horses, raising them and breaking them in himself. Of course he had other achievements that have aided him in becoming a success-ful horse breeder, but this we can state with finality: If he hadn't thrilled to his first achievement, if, instead, he had found horses to be terrifying creatures, he would not be in his present business today.

One achievement does not make a career, or even indicate the direction it might take. It is merely a point, and more points are needed before a course line can be drawn to your success. Thus the importance of listing 20 achievements to be used as reference points.

The Key to Success Factor Analysis

Through the listing of 20 achievements you have made a start on what is to grow into a highly rewarding ex-perience. With this list in front of you, you know that more achievements are not only possible but inevitable. But now doubt creeps in. If you have experienced all of these achievements, and still haven't made a habit of success, of what value are more achievements?

Up to now, as a survey of your list will show, your achievements arrived at unplanned intervals. That is not to be wondered at. Without clear objectives in mind, and with no chart to be used for reference, the results may seem to add up to little for one very good reason; they were never added up. Nevertheless, certain values are there, undiminished by weeks, months or years. Now to chart them and add them up so future achievements will arrive with regularity, and become a habit.

Out of your list, pick the ten that mean the most to you, your ten greatest. Now from your new list of ten, pick your greatest achievement and mark it Number One. Do the same with the remaining nine, numbering them in order of their importance to you. Take your time. Many years of greater success rest on the few hours you spend discovering yourself now.

An achievement is a composite of many things—talent, aptitude, attitude, and even instinct—as in the case of a client who leaped into an ice-choked river to save a child without even considering the fact that he couldn't swim. So now we must analyze your achievements in terms of their parts. Start with Number One and describe it. Write down as many details as you can easily recall. You probably will not have to strain your memory for this.

Here is an example from my files as it was written by a man who is now a top executive: "When I was hired as a Time Study Engineer, the plant was getting an average production of 400 units weekly with a work force of 10 supervisors and 80 bench workers. By means of meetings, organizational work, gaining recognition for the supervisors, etc., I was recognized by the supervisors as their superior—while not yet promoted to that capacity. Within two months management promoted me to Plant and Production Manager, telling me they had no alternative since I was doing the work anyway. I was 28 at the time, and the youngest man in the plant by far. Six months later, using the same facilities and work force, we were producing 850 units weekly. The product was also of higher quality, and morale throughout the plant was much improved. The result was accomplished by reorganizing existing departments, by obtaining teamwork, by installing production incentives, and mostly by making supervisors feel they were important components of the management team."

We will return for a detailed analysis of what he, at the time, considered to be his greatest achievements. In the meantime, with that example before you, describe in about the same detail each of your ten achievements.

Use a separate page of your notebook for each. Some may have arrived as the result of thorough planning; others, like boating a giant marlin, may have been a combination of acquired skill plus the luck of having the big fish come along. And some might have found you rising to meet a challenge that seemed to arrive purely by chance. Give to each the special attention it deserves, regardless of how unlike the others it might seem.

As you are now about to discover, dissimilar though your achievements may be, in them are to be found certain factors that crop up often enough to form a pattern. At the end of this chapter you will find a chart listing the 52 factors that appear most frequently in the lives of successful men. The ten columns provided with the chart, numbered from one to ten, are for analysis of your ten greatest achievements, already numbered in order of importance.

We start with your greatest achievement, proceeding down Column One and consulting the list of factors at the left. What factors appear most sharply in your achievement? Did it involve analysis of a problem? Artistic talent? Ownership, words, figures, memory, showmanship, systems-procedures? The list of factors is not meant to be limiting, so add some more of your own if they seem to have a more direct application. Place a check in Column One next to those factors that apply most directly to your achievement. If, for instance, your achievement was the creation of an effective display advertisement, you could check such factors as creative, design-art, ideas, showmanship, words, writing, and perhaps others. If it was a record-breaking ski-jump, you could check energetic, observant-attention, outdoors-travel, persevering, and showmanship.

In that previously mentioned case of the time-study engineer, he checked the following success factors: things, people (getting along with others), leader, production-controls, organizer, human relations (getting many people to get along with each other), figures (incentive pay), systems-procedures, problem solving, words (meetings), and then added as an extra factor, teamwork.

His had been a production job, a "things" job facilitated by his ability to get along with people. In his analysis of the success factors involved, he had been quite justified in adding teamwork as an important factor. You will notice also that he combined two factors on the list, controls and production, to describe production controls as applied to his job more accurately. At the same time he omitted to check quality and drive, two factors that were certainly important to his achievement.

You, too, will probably be omitting factors in your

first efforts to analyze your achievements, just as I hope you will be able to add factors not on the list. Continue by checking in the second column the factors that figure prominently in your second greatest achievement. Don't rush yourself. In sounding this warning I am reminded of a lady client who admitted, "When I saw my success pattern forming before my eyes, I got so excited about finding out who I was that in my rush to finish I guess I checked out the wrong person."

You will find the same thrill in seeing the same success factors appear in one achievement after another, but this can lead to a pitfall I described earlier as "statistical hypnosis." Having seen a factor like imagination checked in five achievements, you begin to look for it in achievement No. Six, and could have just enough imagination to find it there even though the dominant factors are budgets, controls, and figures. What you must try to maintain throughout the analysis of each achievement is a scientifically detached attitude. For example, imagination certainly could be important to your success. Without it you would not be able to imagine yourself being more successful than you are now, and so would have no incentive to move. But is it a dominant factor, as it has to be in conjunction with such success factors as creative, ideas, design-art, inventive, and their like, or is it only a minor contribution, as in such other factors as figures, memory, and their like?

In all fairness to yourself, check only those factors that are of outstanding importance to the achievement concerned.

Your ten achievements have now been analyzed in terms of 52 success factors or more. Add up the check marks for each success factor and write down the score in the column marked, "Total." Of the 52, some eight or more will register high scores. Within this group of high-scoring factors—four check marks or more—will be found your Success Pattern.

We use the term Sucess Pattern to define the area in which your success factors are most heavily concentrated. Its value lies in narrowing the search for the ultimate in your success. Now we can concentrate on those factors that have produced your greatest achievements and enjoyment in the past, with the assurance that they can be made to do so in the future.

Study now the factors that fall within your Success Pattern, paying special attention to those that have been checked six times or more, or might even have been so dominant as to appear in all ten achievements. As of now the various success factors have been checked only because they applied to a certain achievement, with no effort made to put a higher value on one factor over another. To use our time-study engineer as an example again, he checked 11 factors on the list provided, overlooked two, and added one of his own—teamwork. The check marks gave no indication of the values of the factors, his ability as leader and his ability with figures being checked with the same kind of X.

As the next step I asked him, as I ask you, to go over the success factors and achievements again, this time giving a double check mark to those that were of vital importance to the achievement. He had checked among his factors leader, people, and human relations. Was he a dominant leader, using his lesser abilities in dealing with people and in human relations to support his position, or was he dominantly a gregarious person who found himself in the position of leader because he could get along well with others? It may seem like a small distinction, but it is not. As an amiable person able to work pleasantly with people, he could have made a good boss without raising production or improving the quality of the product an iota. But as a leader, double check mark, he was able to use his other factors of people, human relations and organizer, single check mark, to more than double production, improve quality of product and increase morale.

I might point out that he did not casually put a double check after leader. Always before he had thought of himself as a time-study man, a production man, a pusher. The fact that time-study men seeking to improve the efficiency of labor were not generally loved by workingmen may have accounted for part of his attitude. He had thought he had been able to push through his ideas because of his congenial way of getting along with people. That he was not pushing, but leading had not occurred to him until it was inescapably brought out in an unbiased analysis of his success factors. Since then, recognizing that dominant success factor, he has risen, as already mentioned, to a top executive post with his company.

I want you to use the same unbiased detachment in placing double-checks after those factors that contributed most to each of your achievements. The values of some you may already know. The values of others will require closer study. Some, like discovering that the old and loved portrait of Grandpa on the wall is a genuine Whistler, may come as a complete surprise.

Now then, you have carefully analyzed your success factors and placed double checks after the few that are most important. These we call your Career Directional or Dynamic Success Factors. Unlike the strong factors that determine your Success Pattern, these point to the field in which your opportunities are greatest. The how and why of it will be made clear in the next chapter. But just for the sake of arousing your curiosity, how many of your Dynamic Success Factors are being used in your present occupation? And how much time are you devoting to chores that fall not only outside your Dynamic Success Factors but outside your Success Pattern? Before telling you how to integrate your success factors, suppose you spend another hour or so studying once again the chart you have filled out on the next two pages. Believe me, the time will be well spent. It is yourself and your successful future that are to be found there.

	1	2	3	4	5	6	7	8	9	10	Total
Analysis											
Artistic											
Budgets											
Controls											
Coordination											
Creative											
Design-art											
Details											
Energy-drive											
Economical											
Figures											
Follow-through											
Foresight											
Human relations											
Ideas											
Imagination											
Individualist											
Initiative											
Inventive											
Leader											
Liaison											
Manager											
Mechanical											
Memory											
Negotiations											
Observation											

	1	2	3	4	5	6	7	8	9	10	Total
Organizer											
Outdoors/travel											
Ownership											
People											
Perceptive											
Persevering											
Personnel											
Persuasive											
Planner											
Policy-making											
Practical											
Problem-solving											
Production											
Programs											
Promotion											
Research											
Sales											
Service											
Showmanship											
Speaking											
Systems/procedures											
Things											
Training											
Trouble-shooting											
Words											
Writing											

chapter 5

THE CHART TO YOUR SUCCESS

Discovering Your Real Values

"Never take counsel of your fears," said Stonewall Jackson.

"Attitudes are more important than facts," said Dr. Karl Menninger.

"Act as though it were impossible to fail," said Dorothea Brande.

I agree with all three of those powerful personalities. But how much better if Jackson had suggested some constructive forms of counsel, if Dr. Menninger had defined attitudes, and Miss Brande had listed the actions in which failure is impossible. Before you can act on their advice, you need more information about yourself, and that is to be found in your chart. There is more there than meets the eye.

In mentioning chart reading, I am reminded of my navigator friend who wanted to plot his own course to succeed instead of following the traditional "roads" or "paths." As he put it bluntly, "Before I ever guided a plane across the Atlantic, I studied everything on navigation in the air school, and then everything else I could get my hands on. I studied map reading, and star charts, and instrument analysis, and meteorology. I never worked so hard in my life. I sure didn't want that plane and everybody aboard to get lost at sea, and do you know why? I would be in it."

In the same way, you have as much at stake. Before using your chart to set a course for success, you must know all about it, and all about everything related to it. More work, yes, but fascinating work. It's your chart, and your future success is in it.

In my interviews with clients, at this point I am frequently asked why I deal only with the analysis of achievements and success factors, and not at all with mistakes, failures and their cause. The argument advanced by them is that most of the success books to date recommend knowing your weaknesses as well as your strengths—so that you may make a list of both, weigh them, and if your strengths out-weigh your weaknesses, you're in.

That is a premise about as false as one can find. A weakness results from an absence of strength, and a strength is usually the presence of many strong factors. How can you counter-balance an abundance with a nothingness? Picasso is weak on Einstein's theory of relativity, and Einstein was weak on impressionistic painting. I can assure you that they did not become the most successful people in their fields by trying to counterbalance their weaknesses.

When the mind is sound, only strengths really count, as witness Helen Keller, Franklin D. Roosevelt, and, among thousands of others, my friend Hank Viscardi. Hank, who heads a successful factory and several civic and charitable organizations, refused to believe that his weakness counter-balanced his strength though several agencies to whom he went for help tried to convince him, in the kindliest manner possible, that as a legless man he could hope for little more than charity.

Your weaknesses offer no structural strength on which

to build success. Achievements are solid and dependable; they happened and therefore are quite as real as mistakes. Sometimes a minor failure can be so painful and humiliating that its importance or weight is exaggerated out of all proportion. But how to discover how little of your woe is real and how much imaginary? You can't weigh it to discover if it is large or small, but today we can give you a substantial clue.

In the same way that you picked your ten greatest achievements, pick two or three of your greatest mistakes. Analyze them in terms of the success factors involved. I suggest you do this on a separate sheet of paper that can be destroyed immediately, since you will not want to have it around. Now compare the factors that figure in your "mistake list" with your Dynamic Success Factors. If your analysis has been sound, you will find that your "greatest mistakes" were concerned with experiences that made little or limited use of your strongest success factors. In short, you will find that your greatest mistakes, occurred in those areas where you were stretching yourself thin in a desperate and losing effort to make good.

In that manner you can see for yourself that your so-called weaknesses result from excursions into areas where your strengths can't be used to advantage. The muscle-bound weight-lifter who aspires to be an artist on the flying trapeze, the chess champion who would be full-back with the Los Angeles Rams, and the bank teller who would be a space pilot are traditional examples of what I mean. Yet today they are not as far-fetched as they seem. The weight-lifter might make an excellent catcher in a trapeze act, the chess player a masterful quarterback on complicated plays, and the bank teller a whiz at handling the computing machines and electronic controls that fly our space ships.

No matter what the area in which your Dynamic Success Factors might fall, in today's world of unlimited opportunities, there is a need for them, and unlimited room for your success. How to find the opportunities that are uniquely your own, or how to make them, will

74

be discussed in detail later, but right now I'd like to intrude a seeming contradiction.

Not in your weaknesses will you find opportunity to develop strength, but through some of your strengths you will find weaknesses. By way of illustration, a few years ago I was doing some research work at Sing-Sing in the course of which I met a quaint character, somewhat withdrawn and quiet, but charmingly friendly and incapable of harming a flea. His achievement was that he was one of the best engravers in the world. So good was he, in fact, that he made the mistake of putting himself in competition with the legitimate engravers of stocks and bonds. The forged plates he turned out were excellent, and some, owing to the dominance of his artistic-design factor, were even better than the originals. To the mistake of being too good he then had to add the mistake of spreading himself thin in the areas where his success factors were few and far between. As a solitary artist, he was weak on organization, people, production, sales, systems, and just about every other factor on the list. He was caught when his salesmen, suspiciously unlike Wall Street brokers, offered cut-rate prices on certificates so perfectly engraved that they looked too good to be true.

Should the amiable little engraver read this book and learn how to use his talents more successfully when he is released a few years from now, he will not return to crime. He will have learned that enduring success cannot be built upon a mistake, and that any anti-social or criminal act is the biggest mistake of all. Hence there can be no such thing as a successful criminal. As my research at Sing-Sing proved time and time again, the first mistake—the criminal act—can only produce more and more mistakes until finally, in the confusion of trying to keep matters "straight," the big mistake, or often just a tiny slip, is made that leads to capture or death. Nor can the punishment of a long prison sentence teach a man to profit from his mistake. As penologists are finally discovering, unless the prisoner's honest achievements are recognized and his success factors given a chance

75

to develop while his sentence is being served, he is, upon release, quite apt to repeat his mistakes.

But enough of the underworld where everything is upside down, and careers are based on mistakes instead of achievements. Strengths can still function as weaknesses and lead to set-backs in the world of honest people. For example, a skilled dress-maker in a Fifth Avenue shop could complete a gown so expertly and swiftly that her less-talented co-workers complained she was trying to show them up. When she tried to coach them in attaining some of her own skills, her well-meant overtures were misinterpreted, and she was accused of being "a meddlesome busybody trying to run everybody's business." In the end, to keep peace in the sewing room, her employer reluctantly let her go.

She was a worried woman when she came to see me, hoping I would locate the weaknesses that had caused her dismissal. I didn't have to advise her. By the time she had completed an analysis of her success factors she had discovered the source of her trouble. Of her dynamic factors—creative, design-art, energy-drive, individualist, manager, and production—she commented, "I guess they made me seem pretty bossy. Now that I see myself, I don't blame the girls for not liking me. What I have to do is learn to keep quiet."

She looked at me for a sign of agreement, but I said nothing. Finally she said slowly, "Yes, I see what you mean when you don't say anything. You don't believe in concealing strengths; you believe in using them to best advantage."

She had figured it out for herself, as you can. Today she is the supervisor and shareholder in a large dress-making shop. Her staff is raided constantly by rival firms because of the excellent training she gives her employees. As a highly-skilled supervisor, her "Let's try it this way," enlists immediate cooperation in the same way that, as co-worker, her, "Why don't you do it my way?" created immediate resentment. She doesn't even mind the staff-raiding. "What's good for the business," she told me recently, "is good for us." A happy, well-adjusted woman.

I can also add that because the girls who leave her shop step into top-paying jobs in the industry, she never lacks for skilled replacements eager to do their best for her because of the extra training and inspiration she provides.

Her commendable attitude is being met with increasing frequency but it is far from being wide-spread. As I will have occasion to enlarge upon later, not all supervisors are so magnanimous. If never before has there been so much room at the top, and if never before has the search for ability been more desperate in all forms of business, it also follows that never before have the lower echelons been more reluctant to surrender good men to the top. They need good men, too, and no one in all honesty can tell them that their need is any less pressing than that of their superiors. I am as much in favor of a foreman's keeping a good man on a shovel as I am in favor of a company president's keeping a good vice-president in a secondary position until he—the president—reaches the age of retirement ten years hence. What I don't favor is the man's staying on the shovel, or the vice-president's playing second fiddle if their achievements indicate something better.

Thus it is up to you to know and use your strengths to greatest advantage.

How to Strengthen Your Dynamic Success Factors

Your success factors will respond to exercise in the same way your muscles do. The more you use them, the stronger they will become according to certain well-defined laws. Recent studies by scientists trying to learn why humans behave the way they do show that an individual can, by application, improve any given talent by as much as 20 per cent. Before we can use their discovery, however, we must know what the talent is worth before we can tell what a 20 per cent improvement amounts to. If the talent is zero, a 20 per cent improvement is not going to help matters.

It is here that we can refer to your Success Pattern and

Dynamic Success Factors for an accurate standard of values. Place a value of ten on the success factors checked once or twice, and give increasing values to the other factors in proportion to the number of check-marks. Place a value of 100 on the highest scoring of your Dynamic Success Factors.

Now let's consider the work and the results of improving each factor the maximum 20 per cent. After considerable and often unhappy exertion, the 10-point factor can be raised to an even dozen points. With the same amount of exertion under far happier circumstances, the 100-point factor can be raised to 120 points. The raise alone is worth twice as much as the 10-point factor was to begin with, and the two-point improvement in the latter adds up to a lot of hard work for very little reward.

With those figures before you, the only conclusion to be reached is that your success lies in applying yourself to the development of those factors where the number of points can be increased most emphatically.

To put it more bluntly, if you are in a job that does not require the use of your Dynamic Success Factors but does require, instead, the use of factors low in value, you may work yourself into a state of frustration without making any significant advance. You all know well-meaning, hard-working people like that who have driven themselves to exhaustion to accomplish what others around them are doing with ease. It is these people, too, who often make the most mistakes. In struggling to raise a ten-point factor to the 30-50-point efficiency required by a job, they put themselves under such a strain that mistakes are bound to follow.

In seemingly better shape is the man who uses a 40-point factor on a 50-point job. Through application he can increase his strength to 48 points and thus hold his job without too much strain and worry. The danger here is that in reaching what my previously mentioned executive friends would like to call "his capacity," he may think he has hit his whole peak instead of the peak of one of his weakest factors. In that state of mind he will hesitate to take a better job, feeling that if the present job is tough enough, the new one might be more so.

Not knowing what his Dynamic Success Factors are, he could be right. Should he, as often happens, find himself promoted to a higher job in the same field, his already strained ability could let him down sadly. On the other hand, should the promotion elevate him to a job in which his Dynamic Success Factors could be brought into play, his performance record, his attitude, and indeed his whole life would be vastly improved.

Introducing Functional Self-Analysis

It is one thing to know what your Dynamic Success Factors are and another to use them most effectively. In just what career or occupation do they apply? This is a complex question made attractive by the rich selection now offered to your discriminating eye. Today there are more than 30,000 different occupations or careers in the United States. These can be divided into five broad groups: The commercial world of finance and sales; the industrial world that transforms raw products into salable goods; the service world that teaches, transports, feeds, houses, cleans, etc.; the professional world of scientists, doctors, lawyers, accountants, consultants, etc.; and the ownership world of individual enterprise.

A breakdown of the five groups reveals 12 classifications: Artistic, computing, mechanical-technical, words, persuasion, ideas, science, human relations, problem solving, musical, physical, and leadership.

Here is a simple illustration of how the above information can be used. Suppose your Dynamic Success Factors are words, design-art, ideas, and writing. In combination they point more strongly to the commercial and professional groups than to industrial, service, or ownership, so your attention can be concentrated on those two groups.

Of the 12 classifications, suppose "words" is strongest —that it has been double-checked with several achievements on the analysis chart. Words are essential to both writing and the expression of ideas. Thus the occupation to be sought would be a words job strongly supported by ideas, design-art, and writing. Where is such a job to be found? Advertising, editing, publishing, television, and display printing are obvious fields that come to mind.

Now try to apply your own Dynamic Success Factors as indicated, selecting first one of the five groups and then those of the 12 classifications in which you find yourself the strongest. Maybe the job "made to order" for you will emerge with startling clarity on the first try. More likely further study is needed along the lines that follow. In either case, the advantage of this "success hunt" is that you conduct your trials painlessly on paper and in your mind instead of experimenting for months or years with one real job after another, hoping with blind faith that "This one will turn out all right." Furthermore, I can assure you that when you follow through on the next steps, the results will be more revealing than the months or years of "trial and error" job hunting.

For the next step you need a good public library which carries a comprehensive file of trade and professional magazines as well as books on business and industrial subjects. Here in a few hours of research you can dig up the information you seek on one or more of the jobs for which you feel qualified. Remember that it is your future you are researching, and not some dry subject like the fall of Rome. I might also add that the man who is well read on the current details and background of the company he would like to join is bound to make a favorable first impression when he goes in for his interview. One of the most frequent complaints of employers is that many of their own men, some of whom have worked for the company for years, know little about it beyond the confines of their own jobs.

The procedure you are now ready to start is called Functional Self-Analysis. The name was coined in 1948 by Walter Rust, Placement Director of the Harvard Business School, when we were working there together on a Placement Seminar. Under that name the procedure has become a part of the program I have been developing over a period of years, and was recommended to more than 40,000 alumni of the Harvard Business School.

Much improved in recent years, Functional Self-Analysis now enables you to determine how effective you have been in the past, and how much more effective you can be when you function in a job that uses your best talents to best advantage. Through the discovery of your Dynamic Success Factors you know where and how you were most effective in the past. Through your library research you learn about the component parts—or functions—of a job, and can then relate these functions to your experiences and success factors.

To provide a pattern for your research, I will "functionalize" three typical jobs. First, write down a description of the job, providing as many details as you can from what you have learned of it. This is important, just as it was important that you write down the details of an achievement before you could analyze it.

1. SECRETARY: A position which requires accuracy, speed and neatness in taking and transcribing dictation of letters, reports, statements and meeting remarks. Also required is the ability to maintain orderly records and files, an ease in dealing with visitors by telephone or in person, and poise in dealing with superiors.

FUNCTIONS—six or more: Words—writing, speaking; filing; organization; technical requirements—shorthand and typing; neatness; poise.

2. ACCOUNTANT—OFFICE MANAGER: Supervisor of busy sales office, including eight girls and credit manager (assistant). Customers' orders are received and processed, likewise salesmen's reports and orders. The office handles billings, salaries and financial records under the direction of the Treasurer. The Office Manager is expected to prepare monthly balance sheets for the auditor. He will have a free hand in regard to systems and procedures, providing innovations do not increase costs and lead to greater accuracy, more meaningful facts, and lower budgets.

FUNCTIONS—six or more: Management (leadership) and organization; systems and procedures; personnel; re-

port writing; budgets and cost controls; problem solving.
3. FOREMAN, machine shop: Responsible for supervising the production of twelve machine operators; also, inspection, maintenance, personnel and materials handling. FUNCTIONS—six or more: Planning and organization; systems and procedures; trouble shooting; training personnel; cost reduction; production management; quality controls.

The previous examples show three different job descriptions, and how they may be broken down into six or more segments or functions. Now for the related self-analysis.

Before giving you these instructions, here is why I use the term—"related" self-analysis. Each year more than a million people all over the United States seek their first jobs. Many of them do not have direct experience in a particular function; where they do have, that's fine. But where they do not have experience, let us say, in selling, how are they to prove that they probably have sales talent?

The way to do it is to use "related" experiences. For instance, a sales job requires persuasiveness, and ability to meet and talk to people—among other things. A high school graduate who was on the debating team, and who had been elected president of his class, could use these experiences to prove his ability to meet and talk with people, and his ability to speak persuasively. This technique of using "related" experiences is particularly valuable to the adult who wants *to change his or her career*, the widow who needs to find a job, the man who is too active for "retirement" and needs to continue working.

It is important to know this principle of "related experiences," because it will help you if your kind of work is automated, or otherwise becomes out of date. It will help you when you need to adapt your talents to meet changed conditions. It will give you added flexibility. When you know this, you will be better able to accept changes, take advantage of them, and even welcome them.

The example of "related self-analysis" that follows reveals how seemingly inconsequential experiences can become useful. When you do your own Functional Self-Analysis, the attitude you should have is this: "My experiences themselves do not tell what I have learned from them; what I really have to offer is the sum of what I have learned from all my experiences. What I have learned is most clearly revealed by how I act when I am doing my best. The results that follow such action are achievements or successes. Consequently, I should associate parts of my achievements to parts of the kind of job I want, if I am to truly show what I have learned and what I can do best."

Two steps in F.S.A. have been demonstrated—first, the job description; second, the breakdown into six or more functions. For the third step, you need six or more blank sheets of paper. One function is written at the top of each page. Below it, write two or more experiences which show your highest level of effectiveness in relation to the function.

Here is how the "secretary" did it, without work experience; it is easier when you have work experience.

1. WRITING—SPEAKING—WORD POWER

A) Always did like to talk to people; member of the debating society at high school.
B) Successful as leading lady in a two-act church play.
C) Won spelling bee junior year in high school.
D) Won statewide American Legion essay contest, age 16.
E) As student government leader, frequently required to act as go-between for teachers and students. It was necessary to listen, understand and make myself understood, and also to get ideas across tactfully.

These examples leave no room for doubt about this applicant's ability to speak, write and spell. The first item, "A," flashes a red light; does she talk so much that she would interfere with others? When this is recognized, there is better possibility that it will be controlled—if there is need to control it. Item "B" also shows good memory. And item "E" indicates the possibility of tact and poise.

2. FILING

A. I'm the lost and found department in my family of five. Everyone comes to me when they lose anything, and somehow I seem to find what has been lost.
B. The last half of my junior year I was a file clerk in the principal's office, and she complimented me on the orderliness of the files.

3. ORGANIZATION

A. As co-chairman of the senior prom, it was my job to make all the arrangements and follow them through to completion. I was told that it was the smoothest-running prom we ever had.
B. Can't think of anything else.

4. SHORTHAND-TYPING QUALIFICATIONS

By test, I type fifty words a minute, and take shorthand at 110 words a minute. I am known to be particularly accurate, and make very few mistakes in typing or transcription. With practice, I feel sure my speed will pick up.

Please note the attempt at an apology here, in the previous sentence. Functional Self-Analysis is concerned with results, not excuses. Apologies are not helpful at this time, especially ones which can lead to self-confusion.

5. NEATNESS

A. My accuracy in typing, and my good spelling, help to insure neatness. I had top marks for accuracy during my last three terms.
B. My main hobby is sewing, and I have been complimented on two dresses I made and wear. This shows that I give attention to arrangement or design of things.
C. My report on the senior prom won third prize in the State for appearance and arrangement.

6. POISE

A. Student government leader: This job requires me to be able to get along with all kinds of students, as well as with teachers and some V.I.P. visitors.
B. Senior prom co-chairman: Many times I wanted to blow my top when things went wrong, but I realized that wouldn't do any good. So I just went ahead and did the best I could, and it worked out all right. I believe that needed poise.

This example has shown how experiences that many people would think have little importance, can be used to help determine one's qualifications for a particular job. You will notice that one achievement may be used to support two or even more functions. It may also be obvious that a bit of weakness shows up under No. 3, Organization. If weaknesses were shown in several functions, this paperwork "experience" would disclose whether it would be necessary to think of a different type of job, or modify the job description to exclude the weak areas.

Even when you know what your strongest talents are, when you know your Dynamic Success Factors, and the occupation for which you are best fitted, you will have problems to face, difficulties to overcome. You will need to know techniques that bring you the recognition you should have in the way of promotions, titles and money. You will need to know how to play office politics constructively (please don't shudder; the clean and effective techniques will be described later). You will need to know how to overcome lapses in your self-confidence (next chapter). And you may need to know how to change jobs. All of these can be done more effectively, now that you have come to know your best talents and other qualifications.

chapter 6

YOUR POCKET GUIDE TO
DAILY SUCCESS

Confidence On Tap

How would you like to manufacture "a success?" How would you like to have a "success reservoir" into which you could dip whenever you feel low in spirit or have the "blues?" Just follow the instructions, and you'll manufacture "a success," and build your own "success reservoir."

When most of us think of success, it is in terms of a desirable but nebulous something to be achieved in the indefinite future. "Someday, when I have the time and the money," runs such thinking, "I'm going to have—" and on continues the dream, each to each man's taste.

The distant goal, the long-range objective, is essential to successful career planning, but the lapse of time alone is not going to get you there. Decision and action are the allies of progress; procrastination is the enemy of progress. So time can become an ally of procrastination; for the more time you give yourself to reach a goal, the more time you have to invent excuses for not getting there—and there is nothing procrastination serves more obediently than a good excuse.

How often you have told yourself of the many little things you could accomplish if you could get around to it. Those little things could be "seed" accomplishments. They can be left to die on the vine with no apparent loss suffered, or they can be made to flourish to the enormous enrichment of your entire life.

Only a very little seed is needed to grow a big tree. While this takes a good many years, it is different with people: one little success can start you on the way to very much larger ones in days, weeks, or even hours.

Such seeds could be a difficult apology to the boss or a fellow-worker, with a resulting restoration of good-feeling on the job. The start of a long-postponed reading program to enlarge one's job perspective. The clearing of the top of one's desk to see what the wood looks like. The deposit of the first dollar to pay for next winter's excursion to the Virgin Islands, dreamed of but never remotely approached in 20 years. Every day a new accomplishment, or something to be achieved within a future so immediate that its day-to-day progress is encouragingly visible.

This is a good place to put in a word for selfishness. I am very much in favor of what I call "intelligent selfishness." This is a Golden Rule type of selfishness. It recognizes that the world around me is not very good unless I get along in it; also, that it's just about the same to other people in regard to their feeling good about the world. By this measure, I am intelligently selfish when I help others to get ahead at the same time as I help myself to get ahead. (Another chapter shows how you can use intelligent selfishness to help you get a salary increase or promotion.) Intelligent self-love is necessary if you are to "love thy neighbor as thyself." Actually, the only place where you really have freedom to start is within yourself. So, to put it selfishly, you must start with you.

With yourself in mind, then, be sure to plant among your seed successes a few that cater to your intelligently directed but wholly selfish ambitions.

Knowledge of your best self, of how you use your best capabilities to achieve your ambitions, gives you control of self-motivating forces having great power. You can apply this motivating power to help you overcome weakness, and enable you to outwit that enemy of progress, procrastination. I know an over-weight man who simply could not force himself to stay on the meager diet ordered by his doctor until he made a self-motivating success project out of it. He dearly loved his home machine shop. He promised himself a $15 machine tool if he stayed on his diet a week. Then, self-motivated or powered, he proceeded to save almost two dollars a day on his breakfasts, luncheons and dinners. In six months he found himself with a vastly improved workshop and waistline, and he had made a habit of proving he could do what he wanted done—with barely a dent in the budget.

What would you like to get done within the next 24 hours? Don't think of some unpleasant chore, like cleaning the basement, when you can just as effectively start out on something pleasant. Think of something that can use the best of your abilities, or improve your mind, like reading the book that you meant to read months ago. Write it down, and then in more detail describe four steps needed for its accomplishment. You now have a method to use in reaching a pre-arranged objective. Take that Step One, and because yours is a short-term, 24-hour project, you give Time no opportunity to stop you with procrastination. The remaining three steps will follow through on the momentum of Step One.

Let me warn you about that first step. It may look easy, and even pleasant, but the inertia of years of "getting along" is hard to budge in the direction of "getting ahead." Time used those years to get its forces of procrastination deeply entrenched. Before you can move you must overcome both inertia and procrastination, but once you are rolling, the rest is easy.

The result can be a revelation. In one 24-hour period you have proved to yourself that what you have done in a small way you can do on a larger scale with practice. Destroyed forever is the theory that success is a matter of "getting the breaks," or that it comes to some people because they are luckier than others. You have made many mistakes, accidentally. This 24-hour experience proves you can manufacture "a success," purposefully.

Now that you are rolling, continue setting day-to-day seed projects, not forgetting to reward yourself from time to time. Remember my definition of an achievement—something you did well, enjoyed doing, and are proud of? That "enjoyed doing" is as important to overall success as it is to the achievements that make success possible. Don't let yourself become a slave to success.

It will help you to do this too: At the end of each day, make a note for yourself in answer to the following question, "What's the best thing that happened to me today?" Even on the worst days, some things are just a little better than others. Make a habit of looking for something that is "best" in each of your days.

Your Pocket Guide

Too often there can be days and even months when doubts rise to over-powering proportions that anything is being stacked up at all. These periods of self-doubt and depression are so widely distributed and common as to earn such descriptions as "down in the dumps," or "good for nothing," or "the blues." At such times your level of self-confidence is low, and your enthusiasm lower.

You cannot feel blue when you have solid self-confidence. But when you have made a mistake, your self-confidence is shaken. When you are asked to do something, and doubt your ability to produce, your self-confidence is shaken. When you don't seem to be able to do what you want to do, you let go some of your self-confidence. When you fear results or conditions, you lack confidence in yourself. Seed successes point the way to strengthened self-confidence. A Success Reservoir, as you will discover, is the means you can use to replenish self-confidence quickly, and overcome the blues.

The first step in re-establishing self-confidence is to recognize that you've had troubles before, and somehow or other you have managed to survive them. The problems do seem to become tougher as you get older, but the survival quality put into you by the good Lord also seems to more than match the problems. Even in circumstances where you might have said to yourself "the worst is yet to come," you know that you have found in yourself the ability to meet those conditions and live on.

The big trouble with the previous paragraph is its tangible aspect. You probably agree with its ideas; but when you have the blues, when you lack self-confidence, those ideas just do not come to mind.

As a realist in career planning, I must meet here a challenge frequently raised by clients still not convinced we are living in an entirely modern world. As one said, deliberately fingering a "good luck" coin extracted from his pocket, "It's all right for you to say that success is not a matter of getting the breaks, Mr. Haldane, but I happen to know better. I got the breaks one time—a broken leg—and three men in the office were promoted over my head while I was out on sick leave. I got the break, and they got the promotions. What do you say to that?"

He had me. Being the right man on the right spot at the right time does have its values, but let's not get the values confused. Compared to all the generations of mankind, in terms of opportunity just being in the world during the nineteen-sixties means that, as no others have been, we are in the right spot at the right time. Being the right men to take advantage of it is something else again. I didn't see that his good luck piece, rubbed shiny though it was, could be of much help there. He insisted that it was.

"Every time I get called into the boss's office, I polish it on my pants leg, and I've had three raises in three years," he assured me. I happened to know that in his company you either got a raise every year or you had reached the end of the line. Nevertheless, I could not discount the fact that the charm bolstered his morale, and that was good.

But if some concrete evidence was needed to bolster morale—something to be touched, rubbed, or looked at—why not something based on practicality? Why a rabbit's foot—which certainly had brought no luck to the rabbit—when a list of one's greatest achievements on a small card could provide positive and non-superstitious assurance that the obstacles one had overcome once could be overcome again? It could boost morale in an incontrovertible way. What had been done once could be done again, and no one could appreciate that more than the person who had done it. It should serve him as a constant reminder that he had triumphed over difficulties in the past, could do so now, and would do so again.

I suggested as much to my client, but he was not in an acceptant mood. I changed the subject. We talked about various things concerned with his work, none of them arousing much enthusiasm. In order to start that spark, I asked him what was the most beautiful, tranquil, soul-satisfying scene he had ever viewed.

He paused for a moment, thinking, and when he began talking, some of the querulousness had gone out of his voice. "One evening up on the east shore of Lake Nipigon, in Ontario—" he began. There followed a description of the lake against a backdrop of primeval forest and red sunset that was almost poetry. By the time he had finished, you could hear the bass leaping in the lake and smell the birchwood campfire. And he was a changed man, looking as restored in vigor as if he had visited his favorite scene in person.

"All right," he agreed then. "It is better to believe in my achievements than in a good luck coin. And it is better to create my own opportunities than let a broken leg cheat me out of them. I'll go to work on it tomorrow."

Then he grinned. "Okay, so I'm working on it right now."

I was still marveling at the transformation that had taken place in my client during the course of his description of the lake. "While you're at it," I suggested, "when you write down your achievements on your pocket card, write down your description of Lake Nipigon on the back. Then if you get really worried or flustered, read the description first to calm yourself, and then read your list of achievements for the confidence you need to go ahead."

The description of a beautiful scene through which you can relive a memorable, spirit-refreshing experience can work wonders in producing the calm you need in facing moments of decision. The achievements provide the confidence. And when you are calm and assured, you are at your best.

Such a card, your portable Success Reservoir, is quite as tangible as any rabbit's foot. It will help to sharpen your mind and talents, and stimulate your most constructive emotions. It deals with things you know about, things completely within your experience, things without any kind of mystery. When you lose enthusiasm or self-confidence, a touch or a glance will help to restore it. "Think on these things," it says in the Bible, "things which are beautiful and of good report." This card will help you to remember always that you have the capacity to rise above your difficulties and be successful again.

chapter 7

THE SEVEN MOST DANGEROUS

FALLACIES

Company Politics—Good or Bad?

"Stay out of company politics," the ambitious new-comer is warned, "or you'll get your throat cut before you know where you are."

It is an old warning with a lot of tradition to support it. The fact that tradition supports it, however, should be enough to make it suspect. Company politics has seen its evil days, and some organizations are still torn with it, but by and large the day when close-knit groups resented each other in general and all ambitious newcomers in particular is drawing to a close. As both the groups and the affected companies have learned in recent years, such intramural skirmishing for prestige and influence did the groups no good while greatly impairing the productivity of the company.

When people get along together, production rises; when they don't, it falls. And when they do get along, you can be sure good company politics is behind it, just as you can be sure the opposite is true when hostility holds sway. In either case, politics good or bad is inescapable. When three people in the same car-pool discuss the company on the way to work, you have a caucus. At the drinking fountain, or during a coffee break, or at lunch, if people aren't talking about their work—playing politics—they just don't care, and that's bad.

Lift Your Horizon

Company politics is here to stay. To close your ears to it is not to remove yourself from politics but from the company. How else are you to know what is going on? And if you don't know what is going on in the company, how are you to know where you're going?

Playing good company politics is easy, informative, and rewarding, and is covered by three simple rules. (1) Say something interesting or constructive about your work. (2) Say something good about your boss, supervisor, or company policy—with sincerity. (3) Keep on doing a good job. If you can't do these after a month or two on the job—if your work is so dull and the company so uninteresting—you are in the wrong job.

Carl Anderson did not believe that. He was convinced that his private life and his work life were two separate incarnations. In his private life he had a home, wife, and friends. He could relax and enjoy himself. But work was to him the serious business of getting ahead on his own merits. To him, friendships didn't count in business. He had read a lot of success stories, and was filled with such theories as "stand on your own two feet," and "don't count on your friends in a pinch," and "no one is more resentful than the friend you've stepped over on the way up." The result was that he made it impossible for himself to have any friends during the most productive hours of his day. He never had lunch with "the boys." Company social activities he avoided like the plague. He politely refused to comment on the well-earned promotion of one of his associates, not wanting to commit himself one way or another. In the meantime he waited for his own hard work and attention to detail to bring him the promotion he felt he deserved.

Well, he had a long wait. Three years, in fact, before he came to me for assistance. Even then, I am sure, he didn't expect to find anything wrong in his attitude. He wanted me to tell him what was wrong with a company that refused to recognize his merits. Three interviews of an hour each had to take place before he was willing to concede that people who work together should get along together.

"You say you have been with the company three years, come next Wednesday," I said. "Who hired you?"

"The same boss I've got today. Except for a couple of cost-of-living raises, I haven't moved an inch," he replied.

Everyone in the plant had received "cost-of-living" raises, but the opportunity was there. "Go in and tell your boss next Wednesday that this is your third anniversary, and invite him out for a drink," I urged. "Thank him for hiring you, and thank him for the two raises. Let him know you are alive, and let him know you know he is a living person. Get some life into your job, even if it takes two drinks."

With some reservation Carl accepted my suggestion. Much to his surprise, he found his boss to be quite a likable person, and I am sure the boss was equally surprised to find Carl possessed some of the warming characteristics of a human being. Next Carl joined the department golf team, which he thoroughly disgraced in the company tournament, and found himself better liked as a human being for it. Six months later, when his boss was transferred to a new plant in Texas, Carl was named as the new chief. Politics? Of course. And where would he, or his boss, or the company be without it?

Being the realist I must be, I will admit that company politics can still reveal its evil side in some organizations. Tom Arlen was one such victim. After 23 years with his company, he had risen to the position of Assistant-to-the-President, and indeed functioned as president during "the old man's" frequent absences. Two sons, both ambitious, served as vice-presidents. Then came the cablegram notifying them that the "old man" had died of a heart attack in Jamaica. Instantly both sons moved to take over. Tom, a good negotiator, stayed neutral.

Tom felt that his responsibility—plus a deep feeling of loyalty to his late boss—was to keep the company going. He refused to take sides as the warring sons fought to line up executives and stockholders for the showdown that would turn the company over to one or the other. When the fratricidal activity was over, Tom was out no matter which son emerged as winner. He was fired for disloyalty by the victor when the actual charge should have been unwise impartiality.

That unhappy result of company politics had not gone unnoticed by rival concerns. Men of Tom's proven ability were scarce, and they were quick to bid for his services. Tom was in no condition to make up his mind. For 23 years—his entire professional life—he had given his undivided loyalty to the company and its president, and that his reward should be dismissal because of company politics had left him stunned. His confidence shattered, he could feel only that if he hadn't made good in his old company, how could he expect to make good with a lot of strangers in a new job?

No man can stay aloof from company politics without feeling the effects, adversely. Such an attitude makes him unaware of the inroads politics can make in his career. Bad politics is based on greed, selfishness, power-seeking, and often prejudice that may be regional or racial in nature. Actually company politics is not the name for it, for the company will suffer irreparable damage in the long run. It is personal, or factional, or clique politics, played for the advancement of the few, and let the company go hang, as it frequently does. Yet it cannot be ignored. If it is to be counteracted intelligently, it must be recognized for what it is, from the lowest man subjected to its pressures to the president of the firm. If one is in no position to combat it—and Tom had felt it was not his right to participate in what was essentially a family quarrel—then one must know what it is all about for his own protection. One's personal success is not to be found where partisanship and bias have more influence than merit.

Once I was able to convince Tom of that fact, and that he could not have "pounded the two kids' heads together as their father would have done," he was ready to consider some of his job offers with more confidence. When he did make his choice, it was a bold one. From the New England company producing hard goods he moved to a South Carolina textile firm as vice president in charge of company relations. His parting words were, "I'm a Yankee going South for the first time to handle company politics, something I've always avoided. My Dynamic Success Factors say I can do it—that human relations factor was something I had taken for granted. And you know what I think of bad company politics. Well, if your theories don't work, you'll hear from me."

I've heard from him several times since, following each of his promotions. Recently he was named to the board of directors of his firm, still in charge of company relations, but of all five plants instead of one. I treasure his story particularly. Here was a man whose 23-year career had been wiped out by company politics, and yet in company politics he has found his greatest success.

Clothes Can Unmake the Man

At the age of 33 Williams was ten years out of college, but he still looked like a college fashion plate from the pages of *Esquire*. He worked in the sales department of an engineering firm, preparing estimates on the costs of steel, equipment and labor for the various engineering projects on which his company bid. His work was accurate, and often his shrewd judgment in the selection of cost-cutting equipment won him commendation from the front office. But commendation was as far as it went. When the time came to really go out and do some selling to put the company across—and incidentally make a nice commission—someone else was selected.

Everything in the young man's achievements, education, and training indicated that he was qualified to be much further advanced in his chosen field. But when I looked at him, fresh and eager, his crew-cut blond hair as neat as the bristles on a brush, his clothes representing the last word from Yale, I was reminded of the old adage, "Don't send out a boy to do a man's job."

I handed him a current issue of *Fortune*, suggesting that he scan the pictures of the executives featured in the various articles. He studied the magazine for several minutes, occasionally pointing out a man he knew or had heard about, but when he handed the magazine back, his face was a blank. "What's the point?" he asked.

"Did you see any executives dressed the way you are?" I asked. It was a delicate question with no delicate way of putting it, so I let him have it.

You could see the chips piling up on his shoulder. "Are you criticizing my clothes?" he demanded.

"Would you go to a wedding dressed the way you are?" I continued, ignoring the chips.

"Of course not!"

"Nor a funeral, nor a formal ball, nor a deep sea fishing trip?"

Somewhat less frostily he agreed that his campus garb was hardly appropriate for those occasions.

"What you recognize then," I said, "is that certain kinds of clothes are appropriate for one occasion and not for others. Could it be that the clothes that make the big wheel on the campus do not make the big executive?"

He was bright enough. He got the point. Realizing that if he was going to compete with grown men he had to look grown-up, he appeared in his office the following Monday looking like a junior executive. And when he looked like one, it is not too surprising that he was recognized as one. Of course the new suit did not make him. Clothes do not make the man. Only ability can do that. But clothes can so unmake a man that ability has difficulty in finding a chance to shine.

This is such an important point that I will illustrate it with another case history. This concerns a 36-year-old Greenwich Village spinster who was left frustrated by both art and life. She wanted to be a member of the Bohemian set and paint in oils, but what she actually did was design packages. Time and again her packaging skill had won national and international prizes yet her income was far below that of rival designers; the reason: she looked like a French scarecrow, and a poor one at that.

She wore a faded beret from beneath which strands of black hair hung limply and unevenly, as though the beret was leaking its stuffing. Her face, except for her dark eyes, was colorless, untouched by the cosmetics for which she designed her most attractive cartons. For a cloak she wore a shapeless French cape, her dress was on the order of a blue smock, and her black lisle stockings and black, flat-heeled shoes did nothing to improve matters.

At our second interview I asked her if she believed in packaging. "It's the only thing to believe in that I have left," she said unhappily.

"You don't act like it," I said. I wanted to say that anyone seeing the way she packaged herself wouldn't believe she could put beans in a bag, but I had to let that go. "I should think that anyone who can package perfume as beautifully as you can would be tempted to package herself."

The tears came on then, and after that the story. She was actually a very timid woman, far more concerned with trying to "belong" than in developing her own personality and career. And since it was the current fashion of her set in Greenwich Village to run around looking like spooks—the fore-runners of the beatniks—she had accepted the garb rather than risk the disapproval of her neighbors, or at least those of her "arty" neighbors with whom she was trying to "belong."

One she discovered through an analysis of her success factors the value of being herself, she was able to see herself as her employers had seen her. Her weird garb had not made her a Bohemian artist in oils, but most certainly it had impeded her progress in the field for which she had real talent. Within a month, a living example of her own packaging skill, she became chief package designer for a large cosmetics firm at a salary commensurate with her talent. And from a new confidence in her voice I gathered her other frustrations were within a fair way of being removed, too.

Good Work Will Keep You There

Did it ever occur to you that as a conscientious and hard-working employee you could be standing in your own way? That in mastering your job to the satisfaction of your immediate boss he is quite satisfied to keep you there? A promotion involves more than an advancement and an increase in salary. A whole series of events is put in motion, not he least of which is that in advancing from one job to the next, you have left your former boss with a big hole to fill. He has to find a new man for your job, train him, and then hope the newcomer will work as hard as you did. At the same time, your new boss is wondering how much training he will have to provide before you become as good as the man you replaced.

Under the circumstances, it is not to be wondered at if your immediate superior is far more interested in retaining your high performance record than in seeing you move on, leaving him with a hole to fill. Many a good man has been stopped cold, not for lack of ability but because of too much. The longer a boss has been in his position, the less he may like to see a disturbance of the *status quo*, and even the most tolerant of bosses can get irked if he thinks his department is being used as a training ground for the higher-ups. That a boss would want to keep his best men cannot be considered a plot on his part to keep his men down, but a perfectly natural effort to keep his own performance record up. You can't cure this situation, but you can save yourself a lot of worry if you recognize it for what it is and take steps to circumvent it. These steps will be discussed later.

Let's Look at the Record

Not all good men are kept down because of a superior's desire to retain his most efficient workers. Frequently a supervisor is so concerned with production problems and keeping up with his paper work that his good workers are the men he doesn't have to worry about, and as long as he doesn't have to worry about them, he can forget them. On the other hand, he does know those who are doing a poor job, and he does have to worry and put in a lot of time with them. Thus he slights his most valuable assets—his best men—to concentrate on his substandard workers. So wide-spread is this procedure that a doctrine of management has developed from it called "Management by Exception." Though the procedure is not intended to penalize the good workers, in its concentration on bringing the poor workers up to par, the good workers *are* neglected in too many instances.

As Irving Wiltse had occasion to discover in a double-barreled way, the boss may know his good men—meaning the men he doesn't have to worry about—and yet remain in complete ignorance of their high qualifications. Wiltse came to us after three years as plant maintenance supervisor, deeply depressed by his "failure" to advance. His first assignment, as was yours, was to make a list of the achievements that had been important in his life. He was in a more optimistic frame of mind when he returned with an impressive list of achievements, two of which concerned contributions he had made to improve maintenance efficiency.

"This is the first time I've ever gone over my life in an organized way," he admitted. "It made me feel good to realize I've accomplished a few things."

On his list Achievement No. 9 had become his greatest. This stated, "I set up a separate maintenance shop in the corner of the plant where we could coordinate the repair work of all departments. We had our own tool crib and repair equipment in one place. Instead of trying to bring the men and the tools to a broken-down machine, we could bring smaller machines to the shop and really do a job."

"Did you think this was an achievement when you got the shop in operation?" I asked.

"Well, not exactly," he hesitated. "Not in so many words. I guess I thought of it as something to make my work easier."

"Did your boss think of it as your achievement?" I continued.

Wiltse bristled at that. "He should have. He was there. He okayed the plans. He saw me install everything."

"Yes, but you were there, too, and they were your plans, and you saw the machines installed, yet at that time you didn't think of it as anything special." Then I made my point. "If you didn't recognize your own achievement, why should you expect your boss to do so?"

He got that all right, but I wasn't through with him. "What about your own crew of maintenance men?" I asked. "Got any good men there?"

"I sure have," he said with pride. "The best in the plant. I cover for them, and they cover for me."

"And your boss covers for you," I said. "And that's what you are complaining about. You can call it covering, or you can call it smothering. The results are the same."

Wiltse was frankly astounded. "I never thought of it that way," he admitted. "I guess I was so busy trouble-shooting for the plant that I never thought others might be having the same troubles as myself."

More to the point, once Wiltse was ready to admit he had done nothing to recognize the superior talents of his men, he had to acknowledge the possibility that his boss might be unaware of his—Wiltse's—potential.

It was another case of a good man's keeping accurate, impersonal records of the achievements of his department while keeping no record of his own progress and development—seemingly because there was nothing to report. In a follow-up session with Wiltse I suggested that he keep a personal record of his development as an aid in the "maintenance" of his own career, reminding him that through his records he knew when to grease his machines, while at the same time he had let his own career run dry.

The matter of bringing these important records to the attention of a superior will be discussed in detail later. It is enough for the moment that Wiltse did so, releasing an unexpected chain of events. His boss, in charge of maintenance, plant safety, and special services, had long been held back from promotion to superintendent of a branch factory for lack of a suitable replacement. Wiltse's progress report provided just the ammunition he needed. And you can be sure that Wiltse, having learned from his own analysis of achievements, had brought up one of his best men to succeed him as maintenance supervisor. [None of this being held back for lack of a suitable replacement for him.]

All of which brings up an important point. The higher you go, the broader will be the view of your superiors, until at the top the view is unlimited. That is what makes big executives big. Not for them is the idea that while they are taking six weeks in Florida their underlings are busy in the home office sharpening knives. Confident in their own abilities, and confident in the abilities of those they have left behind to tend the store, they relax and refresh themselves for even greater efforts on their return. You are not apt to encounter this broadmindedness in your first efforts to make a habit of success, but it is a nice thought to keep in mind.

The "Breaks" Are There for the Breaking

Success stories are filled with anecdotes in which lucky "breaks" played a dominant part. The little opera singer who is understudy to the star, and comes through in great style when the star breaks her leg. The first mate who saves the ship when his skipper has a heart-attack in the midst of a hurricane. But you know the story. You also know that unless that little understudy had spent years in preparation for the role and was fully qualified to handle it, she was thanked nicely for her effort and never heard of again. And you know that the first mate, unless he had seniority and experience behind him, continued his career as a first mate under a new skipper. Yet so firmly planted is the idea that the breaks are all important that when a man says, "He got the breaks and I didn't," we don't think of him as offering an excuse; we think of him as stating a fact.

But we are always getting the breaks. The day doesn't pass but what all of us get a break of one kind or another, such as walking into the office just at the moment the boss is ready to fire the first man who walks through the door. Or like taking a Florida vacation during the coldest weather in forty years. The breaks come in all shapes and sizes, and in all degrees of good fortune and bad.

Of course the man who gets a promotion through a lucky break is more discussed than the man who lost it, bad break of equal import though he had, just as the man who breaks the bank at Monte Carlo is more discussed than the hundreds of men whom the bank at Monte Carlo broke. In fact, the top executive who got there through the breaks is about as rare as the gambler who breaks the bank. In the long run the good and bad breaks will cancel each other out, and the man who waits for the "right chance" to come along might do better buying lottery tickets.

Breaks don't make the man, but a man with a program who knows where he is going can make his own breaks. Most of my clients will agree to that, but in some a curious type of reverse thinking sets in. The reasoning goes like this: "I'm dissatisfied with my present job, but at least I know where I stand. To move to a bigger job involves risks, many of them unforeseeable and therefore dangerous. And with a wife and three children to support, I can't afford to take a chance."

The man with that defeatist kind of thinking is doomed if he does, and doomed if he doesn't. Jobs are like shoes. When they are too small for one, they pinch. The pain shows up in many ways—in dissatisfaction, frustration, chronic illness, and all-too-often a short temper that can seriously disrupt family life. A good salary or a title on the door is of little help if the job is still too small. The man seeking to ease his frustrations in the bar of an exclusive club is separated only by his surroundings from the malcontent seeking to drown his problems in a cheap dive. Both are failures, and the difference is only one of degree. One fails more luxuriously than the other, but the therapeutic value of the luxury is dubious, to say the least.

It is true that you are not gambling with your future if you elect to remain in a job too small for you. It is a sure thing that you are going to lose. But let's eliminate gambling, an unpleasant word unless one can afford to lose, and especially unpleasant when a career is at stake. When you know your Dynamic Success Factors and know how they apply to your next step upward, you won't be stepping up in the dark on that neck-snapping step that isn't there. You'll know where you are going, full speed ahead, and let the breaks fall where they may.

Those Distant Goals Can Strain Your Eyes

Back in 1943 a bomber pilot trained in sunny California got his plane and crew as far as Iceland where the weather is more variable at hundred-yard intervals. The next morning he managed to taxi his plane through a blizzard, but when he got to the runway for his take-off to England, he had to call the control tower with the information that he couldn't see half way down the runway.

"That's all right, you're cleared for take-off," assured the voice from the tower. "When you get half-way down the runway, you'll see the other half."

The long-range plan is like that. The pilot of the plane had to have England as his long-range destination, but he could have been stopped far short of there if he hadn't been able to look at it a few hundred yards at a time.

106

The more you concentrate your gaze on a distant goal, the more apt you are to stumble over something right under your feet. The career diplomat who favors a top post in South America is on the right track, but first he should set his eye on learning Spanish and Portuguese, and history, and economics, and politics, plus a plain ability to get along with people before that distant goal comes into focus. Remember what I said about planting seed successes? Use the distant goal as a reference point, but pour plenty of salt over the old adage, "Hitch your wagon to a star, keep your seat, and there you are." The achievable goal you set out to reach within the next 24 hours is the one that gets you there. Unless the immediate goal is reached, with more attainable tomorrow and the next day, the distant goal remains just that—distant. A strain on the eyes and the hopes.

In Summation

(1) It is a mistake to believe your supervisor knows what you are doing, unless you are doing it wrong. Then he'll know soon enough, but superior performance quickly becomes expected performance—"I don't have to worry about that man." To reverse an old saying, "Out of mind, out of sight."

(2) It is an error to keep your work and your life in completely separate compartments. You have a life of your own, but colleagues can be friends.

(3) Dress the part. The "package" makes the first impression and it should be a favorable one.

(4) It is almost tragic to overlook the constructive side of office politics. If you don't know what's going on around you, no one is going to know you are around.

(5) It is a mistake to believe that the time given to an analysis of your mistakes and weaknesses is not time robbed from the development of your strengths and best talents. Talent is what you have to sell. Mistakes, no matter how thoroughly analyzed and presented, have small market value.

(6) It is a mistake to believe you can get ahead without keeping records of your progress. Even the small storekeeper rings up a five cent sale. You, with a career at stake, cannot leave your future to guesswork anymore than the storekeeper can leave his charge accounts unrecorded and hope everyone will pay in full later. And until you keep a record of your achievements, you won't know whether you've collected on them or not.

(7) It is a mistake to have long term, reach-for-the-stars ambitions if you don't have some short term, achievable goals in between. Nothing succeeds like success, and the rocket which, at present writing, is observing Venus is not one big blast-off, but the accumulation of many lesser successes that began with the invention of explosives. (Here again, I might point out, the sole interest is in the achievements of the survivors, and not in the mistakes of the thousands who blew themselves—and a considerable number of innocent bystanders—into fragments.) In short, to achieve the long range success, short term successes must be provided to develop the habit that makes the big one inevitable.

So much for the fallacies and the mistakes. They have the power of out-moded but traditional thinking behind them, and so must be recognized for what they are. Now let's get on to uncovering in the next chapters what to do about circumventing them.

chapter 8

BUILDING SUCCESS INTO YOUR THINKING

Thinking Rich

I know a man who was preparing to change jobs. He expected the new position to bring him an increase of thirty per cent, from $7,200, to $9,600 yearly. His plan was made, his program worked out, and his first steps taken. To put himself in the right frame of mind, he took his wife out and "had a ball." He bought her a "silly" hat she admired, bought himself a fancy tie he wanted, then they went out to dinner and dancing. This is the way, he told me, he had expected to celebrate *after* he had the job. But this time he thought that celebrating ahead of time might give him the feeling of success, and thereby help him to achieve what he wanted. Thinking "rich" worked.

You can see the "think poor" and "think rich" ideas at work in children. Some boys of the same age want roller skates and others want bicycles. They may want them as aids to playing with friends, aids to making money, or merely because other children have them and they want to "belong." Both may have to work for their equipment. The boy who wants roller skates so it will be easier for him to deliver packages is thinking in a very different way from the boy who wants a bike so he can deliver packages to more people in the same time. One boy is thinking in a limited way, only about himself; the other is "thinking rich," about an expanding world and opportunities to be of service to more people.

The T. Eaton Company of Toronto, one of Canada's great stores, was founded nearly a hundred years ago by one Timothy Eaton, a "think rich" immigrant from Ireland. Young Tim got his merchandising training in the Old Country by getting up at 5 a.m. to light the candles and the stove in the small, gloomy store where he was supposed to work his way up to chief clerk in the course of a lifetime. At 10 p.m., and later on Saturday nights, he could lock the store, blow out the candles, and have the rest of his time to himself. His employer was a man who didn't believe there were enough hours in the day in which to accomplish what had to be done, but he believed in using as many hours as he could.

Tim so thoroughly disagreed with his employer that he hied himself off for Canada at his first opportunity, and in Toronto opened his own tiny store. But he was thinking rich. He was the first to use coal oil lamps to brighten up the interior of the store, and the first to use "illuminating" gas, and the first with electricity. And while his competitors continued to stay open until the traditional hour of 10 p.m. to catch the last, late customer, Tim closed at eight, then seven, and finally six, in the meantime paying his ten-hour-a-day clerks what the 16-hour clerks of his rivals were getting. In well-lighted splendor, his well-rested clerks bustled around selling to well-satisfied customers who could see what they were getting and even see to read what was being weighed up on the scales. By thinking rich, by using everything he could get his hands on to increase service and efficiency, he was among the first of the great merchandisers to prove that it wasn't the number of hours in a day that increased sales, but how you used the hours.

Today, in spite of all of our labor-saving devices, we still hear the complaint of Eaton's first boss: "There isn't enough time for everything that has to be done." We are still looking for some magic time-stretcher, and all too often ignoring the time savers we have.

The System That Worked for Him Will Work for You

We still have the same number of hours he had, and on a man-to-man basis each of us can produce eight times as much in a 40-hour week as the best of his clerks could during a 60-hour week. We are better fed, housed, and clothed. Our nightly entertainment, at the flick of a television dial, provides a range of diversions, from grand opera and Shakespeare to slapstick, that Eaton couldn't experience in a lifetime. We have all of this— riches beyond his wildest dreams—and yet as many of us "think poor" today as did in his time. Why?

It is our old enemy, tradition, again. A few decades of progress can't change traditions made "impregnable" by centuries of inherited thought. During the slow centuries in which our dominant traditions were taking shape, our world-changers were a few conquerors, empire builders, philosophers, merchandising and banking princes, and a thin scattering of scientific geniuses. The rest of us were the millions of the great unwashed, unfed, and uneducated. The gulf between the leaders and the masses was so great that no effort was made to bridge it. Instead of trying to bring the people up to their level, the leaders said, "Be content with your lot." "Let well enough alone." "If you want to keep your head, don't stick your neck out." "A penny saved is a penny earned." Et cetera.

And that kind of "thinking poor" is still with us even though we are now enlightened enough to know that "thinking poor" is poor thinking. Let's look at some of those world leaders. Alexander the Great conquered the world knowing less about it than a present-day high school senior. The Rothschilds owned vast portions of the world knowing less about international finance than a good accountant. Any person in the United States has available to him through town, city, and state libraries more information than did all the world leaders prior to the 20th Century combined, and just as much as any world leader of today. As for our own industrial giants like Andrew Carnegie, Thomas Edison, John D. Rockefeller, Jim Hill, Henry Ford, and scores of others, they would, were they to return today, find themselves "educationally undesirable" in their own empires.

Compared to us, those men were poorly informed, and what information they had was often poorly organized, and even more often inaccurate. But they "thought rich," and rich thinking helps to create riches.

Here is another reason for "thinking rich": Though the advances of the last quarter of a century have been called "vast," "explosive," and "overwhelming," every survey by academic, commercial, and governmental agencies indicates that greater advances will be made during the next decade than during the previous quarter-of-a-century. Not only will this open new opportunities that didn't exist a few years ago, but it will create a great need for success-oriented people to match the accelerated rate of expansion. Those who get the leading jobs will be the ones who think rich enough to get them.

The Idea Comes First

Money is only frozen energy. It becomes useful only after you defrost it and exchange it for what you want. The way you think, therefore, influences the way you use money. What you think you want, you buy—assuming you have the money. If you want something enough, you will devote the time and energy needed to acquire the money with which to buy it. By the same token, if you don't want much—if you "think poor"—you will only work enough to get the "poor" things you want.

The late Al Green was a merchandising genius who

"thought rich," but not until he had gone through a shattering experience. At the start of his career he went into partnership with another man. He did very well, but after a year he decided he wanted the whole business so he could keep all of the profits. He knew he was a good promoter whose close attention to merchandising accounted for much of their profits, but in thinking only of his own contribution he was overlooking what his partner was contributing in the way of controlling financial affairs and customer service.

He bought his partner out, and continued to concentrate on merchandising. Because he thought about promoting as the big thing, he worked hardest on that rather than on customer service. Goodwill became non-existent. He went broke. He came to me for job-finding counsel.

Green could not understand how that could have happened to him. He was a man with great pride in his business astuteness, a trait that not only made his failure the more crushing, but also prohibited his seeking help from others. Not until his children began to suffer from the pinch was he forced to recognize that he needed help, something he had never asked before in his life. And help he certainly needed. He had thought so long in terms of profits for himself that he refused to consider at first how he could be profitable to others. Not until he had been helped to understand himself through analysis of his own achievements did he come to appreciate, in all humility, his real worth. Thus encouraged, he did a thorough job of Success Factor Analysis, deciding that he could use his talents to best advantage as a merchandiser of automobile products. Within a week of launching his program, he was offered a job at $12,000 a year to manage a used car lot.

I'm afraid my own enthusiasm did not match his when he reported his success. "You've proved that you are worth a ten-thousand-dollar offer," I said, "but you certainly are worth a lot more. Don't sell yourself short on the first offer. Borrow money if you have to, but think rich. Plan another attack, and go after a job that will really challenge your talents—and bring you the right pay for them."

His morale was bolstered and his imagination stimulated; he envisioned a job in which the used car lot would be run in conjunction with a good garage in which customers could get guaranteed service and related products could be merchandised. Two such jobs he uncovered within two weeks, the second of which he accepted at $14,000 a year. What is more, having discovered the value of service and goodwill, he promoted enough new business for his employer to bring in profits in excess of a hundred thousand the first year. His bonus—another $18,000, for a total of $32,000. Had he thought poor, he might have sold himself short to the first man who offered $12,000.

Success Therapy

Another illustration concerns a woman who had thought poor all her life. She was the daughter of an immigrant who had slaved to put his son and daughter through college so they would have the opportunities he couldn't have. His plan had worked with the son. He had lived up to his father's ambition and his own by becoming a successful engineer. Maybe the daughter had been too close to her father. She saw only his desperate struggle to put her through college, and remembered only her own efforts to scrimp and save by wearing old clothes and eating the cheapest meals so as not to be a burden on him.

Her one period of happiness followed her marriage to a school teacher on a sub-standard salary. Upon his death in an accident, she was left with a five-year-old daughter and a two-year-old son. The insurance policy was almost too meager to contemplate. That was the blow that convinced her that she was doomed to poverty for life.

Some of her story I got from her brother. "I wanted to help her," he told me, "but she insisted I needed my money for my own sons. Finally I sent her thirty dollars, and to make sure she didn't think it was charity, I insisted she take the kids to the finest restaurant she could find for a real banquet. I hoped dining in a nice place would cheer her up and give her something pleasant to remember for a change. Know what she did? She took the kids to the Automat, and then cried for a week because she couldn't afford to do better for them. The funny thing is, she works on old-clothes drives for the poor when her own kids wear the poorest clothes in the neighborhood. She works on the committees to raise funds for refugees, and for milk funds, and for fresh air camps. I'm in favor of this. These committees need somebody to work for them to help the poor, but my sister seems to have a different approach. Mr. Haldane: that girl works harder at being poor than any human I've ever seen."

Of course I agreed to be of assistance, not knowing I was up against the toughest challenge of my life. She "thought poor" so consistently that she could find only four achievements—her college degree, volunteer pre-kindergarten teaching, her two children. Even when it developed that her college degree qualified her as a school teacher, and teachers were in great demand, she began offering excuses. She couldn't leave her two-year-old son, she couldn't neglect her daughter, their clothes needed constant mending, the house took all her time, and who would do her charity work?

My own thought was that she didn't want to face a classroom filled with well-dressed, happy children, fearing that in comparing them to her own "neglected" two she would feel worse than ever. But there was one field in which she could be of invaluable assistance. In several schools there were "slow-learner" groups in desperate need of the special coaching of part-time teachers.

That was something she could understand. These were children more in need of help than her own bright ones. She began by working two hours a day, soon increased to four when a neighbor proved fully capable of caring for her children during her absence. And she proved to be a tigress at fighting for new equipment and brighter-looking books for her retarded children. A grateful mother wrote to the school board in praise of what she had done for her "slow" son. A newspaper picked up the story and followed it up with a feature article on her work, complete with pictures.

Was she rewarded? At one meeting of the school staff an envious teacher who had never had her picture in the paper in 20 years of teaching called her a publicity seeker. An indignant mother at a PTA meeting used the article as proof that the school was spending more time and money on the "dumb kids" than on her smart one. Her principal defended her work, but that he should have to do so made her worry about how long he could put up with the attacks. Fear and doubt made her nervous, she found herself sleepless at night, and when she came to me again, it was only to tell me my Success Therapy couldn't work for her. She had her mind made up to quit.

"Don't be afraid to accept a little help," I assured her. "You know how much your slow learners need help, and fast learners can't get there without help, either. Now about that newspaper article—your good work is what made it a good article. Did it ever occur to you that newspapers are not in the habit of wasting valuable space on subjects that are not worthy of it? Maybe the publicity created a little envy, and then again, maybe it gave you the support you need to fight harder for your children." At that point I remembered enough from Shakespeare to quote: "Our doubts are traitors, and make us lose the good we oft might win by fearing to attempt."

That restored her courage. "Yes," she said, "and if I don't fight for my poor children, who will?" She was still thinking in terms of "poor" children, but at least she was thinking more richly. She went back to organize meetings and conferences with parents that brought her further newspaper attention. The envy and the carping didn't stop, but it was recognized for what it was, and its power was gone. In another year she was sent as the local delegate to a national convention on the teaching of retarded children, and won national publicity for the work her school was doing. Envy turned to pride in being associated with the school which she represented, and her principal, instead of being the goat, became something of a hero for supporting her.

All told, six years of constant encouragement and even prodding were necessary to shift this lady's gears from thinking poor to thinking rich, but the results were well worth it. Today, recognized across the nation for her pioneering work with slow children, she has made such a habit of success that even her children are infected with it. Thanks to her, many of her students otherwise doomed to become public wards are now useful citizens.

These examples, backed by thousands of others, demonstrate what rich thinking can do and does for your career. It is not that thinking makes it so any more than, in the words of the old song, "wishing will make it so." But success-oriented thoughts, supported by a knowledge of your own achievements and guided by intelligent planning, will certainly make it so.

The Penalties of "Thinking Poor"

I have heard, and frequently, that one of the rewards of being satisfied with one's lot is that at least one has peace of mind. The idea seems to be that if one doesn't strive to better himself, he won't be hurt and frustrated if he doesn't make it.

Quite the opposite is true. Man is a proud creature, but pride, unless it is false, can be based only on achievement. When a man's work becomes so routine that all sense of achievement is lost, pride suffers, and all the platitudes about contentment with one's lot cannot soothe an injured pride. To put it more strongly, achievement on which to feed one's pride is as necessary to the complete man as income on which to feed his family. The corollary of that is that a poorly fed pride means a poorly fed family, with a further loss of pride and a greater increase of worry and frustration.

Worry is a doubly vicious form of mental harassment. It consumes an enormous amount of mental and physical energy while contributing not a thing to one's welfare.

At the same time, like a wasteful disease, it produces "think poor" thoughts that create more room in which worry can expand. I remember its effects on one man whose achievements indicated that he was of management caliber though he was currently employed as an assembly line worker fitting tires on automobile wheels.

"Don't tell me that," he moaned. "It takes all I've got to fit tires on wheels, let alone thinking about tackling a foreman's job."

His was not an unusual case. Many men seem to feel that by using only half their talents on the job, they have the rest in reserve, like an army that has half of its men on the front line, with the rest in reserve to be called up in emergencies.

Not so. There can be no half-way measures with success. Talent unused is talent wasted. One might as well say that the Olympic high jumper should practice with the bar set at three feet to keep his talent in reserve for the great day when he will be called upon to jump seven feet six inches. With his muscles subdued by that kind of training, he'll never make it, and with your best talents subdued by "think poor" thoughts, neither will you.

Here is what actually happened to John Carleton, a married veteran who went through college on the G.I. Bill of Rights. His second child was born during his senior year, and he was one proud graduate when he posed in his cap and gown with his wife and family. Then at a graduation party that night he was brought crashing to earth by a statistically minded fellow graduate.

"You know, John," this realist informed him, "I've figured it out. By the time your two kids are ready for college, it will take fifty thousand bucks to put them through, and no G.I. bill to help. As a matter of fact, now that we've graduated, we haven't got any G.I. bill to help us any more."

For three years during his Army career, and three more during college, John had never had to worry about where the money was coming from. It was not much money, but at least a regular income. Now, all of a sudden, he saw himself confronted with a $50,000 debt, and it over-whelmed him. He had tentatively accepted a teaching job in a small town high school, but it no longer looked adequate for his needs. The higher paying job with a wholesale house that he had turned down as "too drab" had already been filled. He scurried around hunting for the "big money" job he thought he had to have, only to discover that the big companies had signed up the college graduates they needed during the same period he had signed up to teach school. He was out all the way around.

During the summer months he did uncover a few possi-bilities, but each job had something wrong with it. The starting salary was too low, there was no room for rapid advancement, it wasn't his kind of work, it was routine work beneath the dignity of a college graduate—always something. His subconscious mind had frozen on the $50,000 debt he saw hanging over him. When no job promised him that much—and no job can promise that much until you can promise that much to the job—his morale dropped to zero. He moved his family into the home of his parents, blaming his plight on "the recession" that was purely one of his own "thinking poor."

With John still jobless in November, his father told him firmly that if he wanted to give his children any Christmas presents, he would have to earn the money himself. "I'm taking care of you," his father told him, "because you are part of the family, and your children are my grandchildren. But I'll not buy gifts for the kids and have you sign them to John and Kate from daddy. That would make liars out of both of us."

Thus stung, John got his first job as a toy salesman in a department store, one of the scores hired for the Christmas rush. To say he was thinking poor is to put it mildly. "I hit bottom," he told me later. "There I was, a college graduate, and a lot of high school kids were filling in for the rush at the same salary. Doing a better job than I was, I have to admit, because they were eager and I wasn't. I couldn't stand that, having kids ring up more sales than I did, so I went to work to top them. I did, too, but I couldn't take any pride in it. Beating kids."

Not until John saw the pleasure of his children in the gifts he had bought with his own money did he really snap out of it. "I thought then that maybe I wouldn't be able to give them much, but at least they'd enjoy what they got," he said. "I stopped worrying about their college educations, and started worrying about buying them clothes for grade school."

If he was still worrying and thinking poor, he had freed his subconscious mind of the $50,000 debt. He was ready to analyze his achievements in a more constructive light. He was even ready to plant some small seed successes instead of trying to "shoot the works" for an unrealistic $50,000 job. He was prepared, in other words, to make his climb towards success one step at a time.

The first thing an analysis of his achievements did for him was to restore his morale. The achievements were real. They represented things he had done well, and which had rewarded him with a feeling of pride and accomplishment. Each achievement represented a "think rich" situation. On the basis of that kind of constructive thinking, he determined that advertising was the field that could use his achievements to greatest advantage. We worked out a program through which he got a job in the advertising department of the store in which he had worked during the Christmas rush. Since then he has become Advertising Manager, and his future and the education of his children are assured.

Unconscious Attitudes

John's case is not an exaggerated one. All of us suffer from fixations (like his "$50,000 debt") that cause us to freeze in the face of the enormity of the thing instead of looking for the ways to cut it down to size. Your brain creates these fixations when it is conditioned by "think poor" thoughts, and will just as readily banish them free of charge and with little effort when you train it to "think rich." As we know today, there is no trick to setting up a mind-training program. Part of your brain is always working—on regulating your heart beat, your breathing, digestion, and other automatic functions. This subconscious part of your mind also responds to commands from your conscious mind, enabling you to walk, run, drive a car and perform all the routine tasks of living without having to concentrate your mental powers on every step, turn of the car wheel, or blink of the eye. But the greatest, and most misused, function of the subconscious is to collect all your experiences, evaluate them, and file them in your memory for future reference.

At some time or other, when faced with a knotty problem, you have said the equivalent of "let me sleep on it." And if you actually did sleep on it, feeling strongly that you would have the solution by morning, the chances are good that you woke up with the answer. Your conscious mind, before losing itself in sleep, had transferred the problem to the sleepless subconscious mind, commanding it to produce. Of course, if the facts on which to base a conclusion are not stored in your memory, no solution can be forthcoming, but if the facts are there and need only correlating, your subconscious can and will produce, sometimes with such startling suddenness as to wake you out of a sound sleep.

It is this mysterious obedience of the subconscious to the commands of the conscious mind that only recently has come to be appreciated. Now we know that if the conscious mind "thinks poor," the subconscious responds in the same low key. If you think you don't have time to do all that must be done, if you feel that you are a hard-luck victim for whom things always turn out badly, your subconscious will influence your conscious mind to waste time on projects that are bound to turn out badly. Conversely, if you "think rich," this same subconscious will go to work with enthusiasm, slaving away for you even while you sleep.

The readiness of your subconscious to go to work for you is one of the great discoveries of recent years. The subconscious has been so long cloaked in Freudian words and symbols that a belief exists that it has some immutable identity of its own, probably bad, and the least said about it in polite society, the better. According to that belief, your "think poor" thoughts are dictated by your subconscious, with your conscious mind being the unwilling victim. Recent tests have not only disproved this belief, but they have demonstrated quite the opposite. You can change your subconscious mind as easily as you can change your conscious mind, and once changed and put on the right course, it will work tirelessly to follow through. So subservient is it, in fact, that it will even learn a foreign language for you while you sleep. With an earphone planted beneath your pillow, and a tape recorder repeating the lesson over and over, you dream your way through Spanish, French or whatever, your conscious mind pleasantly soothed by the words your subconscious ear is absorbing, and the lessons learned by the subconscious are there for the conscious mind to command as surely as the lessons learned in a classroom.

What this means to you is that when your conscious mind makes a habit of success, your subconscious mind will also make a habit of success, awakening you every morning with "think rich" ideas and answers. When it is conditioned by "think poor" thoughts, your subconscious drags you out of bed to go "back to the salt mines," already defeated before the day begins.

What this boils down to is that either you put your subconscious to work with "think rich" ambitions, or it will enslave you with "think poor" goals. It has no ambition of its own. It is lazy, and will seek the path of least resistance. Only your conscious mind can determine what you want out of life, and guide your subconscious accordingly. And once it has been mastered, it becomes the obedient servant that works day and night to help you achieve your objectives.

One other point. Your subconscious mind can be commanded, but it cannot be deceived. When you set unrealistic goals, as John Carleton did with his $50,000 job that he wanted "right now," the subconscious recognizes the futility of trying, and either gives up or replaces practical work with wishful daydreams. Then you freeze, or have fantasies, and become powerless. When you do know what your achievements are, and know how they relate to your future, and when you plant seed successes that lead to quickly attainable goals, your subconscious will back you all the way, and help you make a habit of success.

chapter 9

HOW TO GET THE JOB
YOU WANT

Growing Pains

Dr. Norman Vincent Peale likes to tell the story of the old gentleman whose greatest claim to fame was the arrival of his hundredth birthday. At the party celebrating his accomplishment, a reporter lured the centenarian into conversation with, "You must have seen a great many changes in your lifetime?"

"I sure have," replied the spry old gent, "and I've been against every one of them."

In his resistance to change, the old man differed from many of us only in that he had worked at it longer. All progress is based on change; all change is by tradition painful to some degree, and hence to be avoided. Change is described in such terms as "breaking" with the past, "tearing up old roots," and "losing old friends." Painful descriptions, most of them, leading many to yearn wistfully for the good old days, which were not necessarily so good at all.

One real estate developer building houses in the $65,-000 bracket found his success-conditioned clients wanted all the latest improvements, which he had, but his houses didn't really start to sell until he ornamented them with old brass coach lamps, wagon wheels, and similar symbols of the past. Later he discovered a fad among his buyers of hanging old oil portraits of alleged ancestors in the split-level living rooms. In their new and rootless community, the newcomers were trying to find what comfort they could by creating an artificial past of their own. They wanted change, but they also wanted a past to cling to, even if they had to make it themselves.

I can approve of their actions, wistful though they might seem. The instinct to cling to the past, to what is known, to habits that are as "comfortable as an old shoe," is a powerful one, not too far removed from the infant's desire to cling to mother. To tear one's self away, to go out into the "cold, cold world," requires a determination that not everyone has.

There is, however, another instinct as powerful as the desire to cling to the past, and that is man's instinct to better himself through his achievements. Achievements stimulate progress, progress accompanies change, and change involves risks which might be painful. Sooner or later, in every man's career, the two instincts clash. To strive for greater achievements, or to cling to what one has, that is the question. And instincts can't answer questions. Only intelligence can do that.

Grandpa could say of his ancestry, "What was good enough for grandpa is good enough for me." He would suffer no loss of status in making that statement, because his achievements would be pretty much what his grandfather's had been, and maybe a little bit better.

Today such a statement is no longer acceptable. Progress is no longer a slow matter of evolution, but a manufactured product on a high-speed assembly line that produces by the hour what our ancestors did by the century. Change comes in such an uninterrupted flow that painful or not—a score of jobs held for 20 years become obsolete in the face of an automated machine worked with one finger by one man in a white smock—it has become a way of life. A more complex way, I'll admit, but it is here.

The net result of high-speed progress is that the instinct to cling to the past offers few rewards except to dealers in antiques, while the instinct to better one's self through achievements has at last been freed of the shackles of tradition. And never in history has the world been more eager to reward achievements. It has to have them. And so do you.

The first steps, until success becomes a habit, are the hardest. By now, through analysis of your achievements, and through Functional Self-Analysis, you know what you will be able to do best, and what will be best for you. The first step up may mean a promotion in your present department, a transfer to another department where you can exercise your talents with greater freedom, a move to another company in an entirely new field of endeavor, or possibly the establishment of your own business. Or it may involve getting your first job, and you want to be sure it is one that will provide valuable experience you can use later.

There are a lot of ways of making an approach to a promotion or a new job, and these will be dealt with at length in later chapters. First let me give you some background facts to serve as a guide.

Less than five per cent of the jobs paying more than $900 a month are filled through employment agencies. More than 80 per cent are filled through the recommendations of friends already employed by the concern, or through "contacts"—"Uncle Joe is a friend of the boss"—or through tips that "so-and-so is in need of a 'willing worker.'" The remaining 15 per cent or so of jobs are filled by responses to "help-wanted" ads, or through letters of application sent to firms with whom the applicant hopes to be associated. In almost every instance, however, the formal process involves an interview, so let's start with that.

How to Conduct a Job Interview

The above heading may seem strange, since you are the one being interviewed, and the man who holds your fate in his hands should be the one to conduct it. Unfortunately, as I know only too well, most job interviews, when conducted by the man with hiring power, show little improvement over the days when men stood outside the gate of the employment office and were selected by the breadth of their shoulders and the strength of their backs. He is still thinking the same negative thoughts. If he doesn't hire you, you can't be a discredit to his judgment. If he does hire you, and you flop, he will get the blame. Far easier to let you go, and hope the next man shows greater promise.

It is up to you to be that "next man" with the greater promise. Through Functional Self-Analysis you know what you have to offer, and you have the assurance that you can do the job well. Your prospective employer knows nothing, or very little about you. This puts him at a disadvantage. I might add that this is one of the primary reasons why most job interviews are conducted in a strained or uncomfortable atmosphere, so much so that some people come to dread them, and get the jitters hours before the meeting. This unsatisfactory situation is worsened when the applicant is just hoping to get a job with the company, knowing little of what job openings there might be, and still less about his ability to fill them. Then you have two men sparring in the dark, and one can well understand the complaint of the supervisor man who cried, "I had to spend all day interviewing twenty men to fill one job. Most of them just wanted to get on the payroll, 'Any where you say.' How can you talk jobs to men like that when they don't even know what jobs you're talking about?"

Merely knowing what you are talking about gives you a big edge on most applicants. Bluff won't work. The average supervisor or executive is not to be over-awed by big talk. But the assurance that comes with knowing what you want and why you want it is something he will recognize and appreciate. You have taken some of the discomfort out of the situation, put him at his ease, and provided a meeting ground on which you can get together.

If you are one of the more than 80 per cent who gets his new job through recommendations or contacts, these same sources may be able to provide the background information on the work and the company that you will need for ammunition on your first interview. (I am assuming, of course, that you want this new job because it will provide greater release for your Dynamic Success Factors, and that you have fortified your verbal information with outside reading on subjects related to the job and company.) It is also possible that your friend or contact in the company has served to put your fateful interview on a more cordial basis than that accorded strangers.

But before going on with the conduct of the actual interview and the psychological factors involved, let's begin with the case history of a man who said he didn't have a chance, but he wanted to take it anyway.

Tom Strouss was a government agency administrator in Washington, D.C. who, at 43, discovered that he was growing faster than his job. Egging him on was the memory of the six months he had spent in San Francisco during the war. He yearned for the hustle and bustle he had seen there, so different from his slow-but-sure agency in Washington; he yearned for the climate; and above all he yearned to see what he could really do if given the opportunity to use his best talents to the full.

"The trouble is," he told me, "I don't have a friend out there. I was in the Army, remember, so I didn't get to meet any businessmen. I didn't think I'd ever be coming back, so I didn't bother to make a single contact."

"Then we had better manufacture some," I said. "San Francisco is too far for a man to take his wife and children and arrive cold. Let's open some doors before you start."

Yes, you will be glad to know, contacts can be manufactured. They are too valuable to leave to chance. A man's contacts are usually limited to those he meets at work, and those he meets socially after hours, a remarkably tiny group in comparison to the opportunities there are in the world. But as I discovered early in my work, many a man would rather sacrifice his professional growth by remaining with his friends than risk "jumping off into the unknown," bereft of contacts. And having discovered that fact, I set out to see what could be done about it. With opportunities unlimited, and contacts restricted to a few friends and associates, the answer was obvious. Manufacture new contacts where needed, whether they be in San Francisco, Hong Kong, or Decorah, Iowa.

Here is what Tom, following our suggestions, did to open the doors of more than eighty concerns in San Francisco. First he obtained the names from a business index of 100 leading executives. Then he sent them this letter— which I will analyze later—defining the area of administration in which his Dynamic Success Factors could be used most profitably by his employer and himself. This type of letter, written with an assist from me—also to be analyzed—has been proved effective by literally millions of dollars in increased success for clients in the $9,500 to $50,000 income bracket.

The letter follows:

"Dear Sir;
"I have to make a $500,000 decision, so I need dependable information that will help me in coming to the right conclusion. I can't get that kind of information from just anybody; that's why I'm turning to you.
"In brief, I want to know if there may be a need for someone with my qualifications in the San Francisco area. I'm not asking you for a job; I have a good one. I really want your common-sense opinion as a business leader. My desire is to return to San Francisco, but there is no rush, and I will not make the attempt unless success is reasonably sure. Friends have told me about

'plenty of opportunities,' but friends are biased, and I am looking for good business judgment.

"Here, in a paragraph, is my background: I head up a government agency department, supervising some 120 professional and clerical people; there used to be 160, but I analyzed the operations and reorganized the department to do more work with fewer people. I am a good budget man, know accounting, can get along well with—and train—personnel, and have a law degree. I like trouble shooting, and write good reports. At 43, my salary is $18,000.

"If you think a demand for someone with my qualifications might open up in the next year or so, I would further appreciate your advice as to whether it would be best for me to visit the West Coast to look around, or to send a lot of résumés to companies that might open employment possibilities in advance.

"Believe me, your opinion will be helpful at this time, and much valued. I look forward to hearing from you.

"Sincerely yours,
"Tom Strouss."

From the 100 letters, Tom received 81 replies. Of these, 58 were direct answers from the executives queried, all of them constructive, and many of them containing valuable suggestions. The other answers were routine form letters from personnel departments, two of which cautiously admitted that he would be welcome if he happened to be in the neighborhood and dropped around. No letter included the offer of a job. He hadn't asked for one.

I can hear you asking, "What's the point? He wants a job, and all he gets is advice."

The answer is so important that I want to take it up one point at a time.

(1) The worst way to build contacts is to begin by asking for a job. The psychological reaction of a man being "hit for a job," is to go on the defensive, and "No" is his first line of defense. You may think of yourself as an applicant, but to him you are a supplicant, asking him for a favor. His second reaction is one of resentment— "Why is this man bothering me, especially at this time when I have all the men I need?" (Men have been hired

by arriving on the scene at the precise moment their services were needed, but the chances are less than a hundred to one against such fortuitous timing.) His third reaction is one of suspicion—"Who is this man? What's wrong with him? He's probably been fired for some reason." His conclusion: "If you want a job, that's your problem, not mine. And I've got all the problems I need without taking on yours."

Those are some of the thoughts running through his mind. What he will be saying to you, pleasantly enough, will go something like this: "With your qualifications you won't have any trouble finding a new job. I'll certainly keep you in mind, and if anything opens up, or if I hear of any leads, I'll let you know. I'll call you."

You have been told "No" in no uncertain terms. And you have lost someone who could have become a good contact had the approach been more diplomatically made.

(2) If you send a letter to an executive asking for a job, he or his secretary is likely to shunt your correspondence—almost automatically—to the personnel department, which generally is last to hear of the really good job openings.

(3) When you ask a man for advice, you compliment his good judgment. And when he gives advice, he will want you to follow it up, and he will want to follow your progress. He has a personal interest in you, because, after all, the soundness of his advice is at stake. He doesn't want to let you down, because, indirectly, your let-down would be a reflection on his advice, and hence an injury to his pride.

(4) You must be remembered in order to be recommended. A "manufactured contact" remembers you because you asked his advice; this is a memory-fixing technique, and so is asking him to consider recommending you to someone else.

Now to return to Tom Strouss. To the 58 San Francisco executives who had written constructive letters, he replied immediately:

"Dear Sir;

"Thank you for your helpful thoughts. I am sure you will want to know when and how my ideas have jelled. I will keep you informed.

"With appreciation,
"Sincerely yours,
"Tom Strouss."

He expected no answers to that letter, and received none. He waited a month, and then mailed the following letter to the 58:

"Dear Sir;

"My plans have jelled; and as promised, I am reporting.

"Starting Monday, January 12th, I shall be staying at the Mark Hopkins Hotel for two weeks. I want you to know how much I appreciate your helpfulness, and I will take the opportunity to thank you in person soon after I arrive. It seems as though there should be opportunities for me there, and also that it would be best if I explored them in person.

"In the meantime should you happen to hear of an opening into which you think I might fit I would appreciate your passing along the enclosed résumé.

"My best wishes to you. I am certainly looking forward to shaking your hand.

"Sincerely,
"Tom Strouss."

Ten days later Tom arrived in San Francisco. He had traveled nearly 3,000 miles. He had no appointments, and not a contact that he knew personally. But he had not been idle during the six weeks between the mailing of the original 100 letters and his arrival at the hotel.

He had followed all of the procedures detailed thus far—from the discovery of his Dynamic Success Factors to a thorough understanding of their applied values through Functional Self-Analysis. He had topped this off with library research in Washington on industrial activity in San Francisco.

I could see his confidence grow from week to week. Except for his Army career, in which he had risen from

132

draftee to first lieutenant, he had worked only for the one agency in Washington, and while his desire to get into private industry was strong, it was almost matched by his fear of taking his wife and children into a highly competitive world in which he had no experience. Or thought he had none, which is just as bad.

The analysis of his achievements was the first boost to his morale. His confidence grew another tall step when he discovered that these achievements could be used to even greater advantage in private enterprise. By the time he left for the West Coast, he knew more about himself and his abilities than most men do. And he knew more about San Francisco and its industrial opportunities than did most of the Native Sons.

Tom had already followed the four points needed to "manufacture" contacts. These are (1) Avoid asking for a position, because it nearly always brings rejection. (2) Associate yourself, make contact, with men in management at the highest appropriate level, and ask them for advice or counsel. These are men in positions of power whose recommendations will open doors to you. (3) Use memory-fixing techniques: Know your best self, and "teach" your interviewer the facts about you that he should pass along to a business friend who does have a job opening or opportunity. (4) Be well informed on your capabilities so that you can speak or write briefly and enthusiastically about your effectiveness.

Your Sales Department

I cannot state too emphatically that self-confidence based on a knowledge of yourself and the kind of job you are going after is an essential if not the most important factor in good job interviews. Tom had found this self-confidence through the assistance of the same procedures presented to you in this book. He knew he had talent for sale. What he needed now were some good salesmen for those talents—executives who knew their way around, and whose names were important enough to open doors in their own right. The alternative—ringing his own doorbells and then trying to get his foot in the door—is one I don't care to contemplate, much used and much favored by tradition though it is.

Tom had these salesmen. The same executives committed to his success by having given him their advice. Not that they were ready to sell him sight unseen. They had not become executives through making deals like that.

Tom telephoned his first man within five minutes of reaching his hotel room. The voice was coolly cautious, but receptive. "I'll be glad to see you," said the voice. "How about ten a.m. when the secretary brings in the coffee?"

"Fine. I'll be there," said Tom. He had lined up his first interview, and thanks to our coaching, he had placed the correct interpretation on the invitation. "I'll be glad to see you," was polite businessese for, "I'd better see you, because I won't make a move until I've had a chance to give you the once-over." The invitation to coffee might have been sheer Western hospitality, but more likely it meant, "As long as we are just enjoying a cup of coffee, you know, everything is informal. No serious business, you understand. If you pass the coffee test all right, we might get around to that later, but for the moment you'll be my guest, and I hope you are not rude enough to try to take advantage of it."

But don't overlook this—within ten minutes of his arrival in town, Tom had his first interview lined up with one of the influential men of the city, and that it included an invitation to have a cup of coffee—well, many a long-term employee in the firm had never enjoyed the privilege of sitting down with the boss under those intimate circumstances.

From Tom's report, the interview while the coffee was being brought in covered his trip from Washington, the view from the Top of the Mark, the climate, the fog, the Golden Gate Bridge, and traffic. Two minutes for that, and then, after the first sip of coffee, the first tentative lead from the executive: "I've read your résumé. Interesting. I didn't know you fellows in Washington—I guess we always think of you as bureaucrats—worked that hard. Tell me something about yourself."

Tom was ready for that. "Would you rather I started in with my background in office systems analysis, or budget development, or office management?"

His voice was casual, but his question wasn't. It was one of many carefully calculated in advance to meet almost any opening lead. The technique he used—and you can use—is designed to eliminate those first awkward moments of indecision. Awkward because the executive doesn't know where you might start, and so can't brace himself in advance, and awkward because you don't know what start might be most effective in winning the executive to your side.

Remember this: Only you know what you want during the first stages of the interview, and this advantage lets you play the first question on your own terms. Tom played it that way by mentioning the three job functions that he did best, and on which he was qualified to speak with authority. But he didn't brag that he was an expert in those fields. His answer implied that he was, but when he tossed it back to the executive, it was with a polite question mark that removed all traces of braggadocio.

Thus disarmed, the executive said, "Start wherever you like. It's your story."

"All right. Office systems analysis. After analyzing our systems, procedures and flow of work, I reorganized our office operations so that we were able to cut our staff of a hundred and sixty people twenty-five per cent, to a hundred and twenty. I found four weekly reports which no longer had meaning or usefulness. These were dropped, and I developed ways to combine others meaningfully so that six became two. A lot of paperwork was eliminated, then I reorganized to further simplify operations and cut costs. . . ." And for two minutes Tom described his duties with no waste. He ended with another question, "Would you like to ask me some questions on that, or would you rather I went into my experience with budgets, office management, or personnel training?"

This question, too, had its purpose. He had talked about himself for two minutes, long enough to make his point, but not so long as to create the impression that he was in love with the sound of his own accomplishments. Then through his question he asked the executive for further instructions while directing the line of inquiry upon his own career. The subtle effect of this was double barreled—it returned the command of the interview to the executive, who otherwise might have begun to get restless had the monologue by a stranger been prolonged, and yet it left Tom in command of the direction the interview would take. He could either answer questions, as he was prepared to do, or he could talk on budgets or managements. The important point here is that no matter which subject the executive pursued, it would be of his choice, and therefore he would be interested.

"Go ahead on budgets," he suggested. "I think you cleared up office systems analysis pretty thoroughly."

Tom took up that subject in the same brief and thorough way he had covered the first. Followed through in this way on three more subjects, Tom was able to put his best foot forward, solidly, during the fifteen minutes usually allotted to the "coffee break." The executive was impressed by both Tom's brevity, and his ability to cover a lot of ground without seeming to be in a rush.

"I'd like you to meet our Controller," he said, standing up to close the interview. "I know he doesn't have anything at the moment, but I know he'd like to meet you. In any case, he'd be the one who would know more about other companies who might have openings than I do. He has to get around more than this desk-bound slave."

Then he called the Controller on the inter-com, and the appointment was made, and for right now. When a top executive sets up the appointment, it usually is for "right now."

Then the interviews really began. The Controller really got down to cases, and it was noon before the interview was ended. Tom felt he had talked himself out, but when the Controller said, "Noon already! How about joining me at our luncheon club?" he was ready. He met eight men in the course of luncheon, and one job interview was arranged then and there. He had been in town 24 hours, had made ten solid contacts, and had one firm job appointment. He still hadn't asked for a job, and he wasn't going to. We had warned him about that. Sometimes the first offer may be the best, but it isn't likely. He had given himself two weeks to shop around, and he wasn't going to commit himself until he had seen what they had to offer.

They were an exhausting two weeks—over 80 formal interviews. All this time Tom had not asked for a job. He asked only to be the means by which the executives who interviewed him could help their friends obtain a capable employee. By not making a direct appeal, he was not subjecting his new friends to the embarrassment of a refusal. Each man was free to consider Tom as a possible addition to his staff, or free to recommend him to a friend—as a favor to both the friend and to Tom.

Now let's examine the psychology of Tom's approach in terms of your own job interviews.

Inside Looking Out

So ingrained is our tradition that a man should start at the bottom and work his way to the top that some sort of a stigma is attached to job hunting. Why, so the thinking seems to go, aren't you working the way to the top with your original company instead of butting into our business? Were you fired, laid-off, or are you one of these restless job jumpers? Or are you a moon-lighter, trying to hold down a day and a night job simultaneously? Except in our youngest industries, like electronics and television, the first challenging question is more apt to be, "Why are you coming to us?" instead of "What have you got to offer that we need?" This only slightly veiled hostility still exists in most industries even though those industries are in desperate need of top-flight men, and even though the executives of those industries realize that many a man's talents are atrophied by the lack of opportunity for growth in their present jobs.

Because of this, the tendency of talented men is to keep their job hunting to a minimum, first because it's a painful process, and second because they don't want to get the reputation of being "floaters" or job hunters. They have no hesitation about trying on shoes until they get a pair that fits, but when the job doesn't fit, and their futures are faced with a permanent pinch, they'd rather keep hoping for the best instead of doing something about it. The result is that they know little about the technique of job hunting, or even that there is a technique.

The same type of thinking affects the executives who need to hire the best men they can get. Hiring a man—buying his life in monthly salary installments—entails an enormous amount of responsibility that increases in direct proportion to the importance of the job.

In the lower levels of employment, where the ability to do the job is the main requirement, the employee either does his work or he gets fired. It's that elementary. The boss might not like to fire him—for most men firing an employee is an unpleasant if not downright shattering experience—but at least he is not to blame if the employee can't handle the job.

But the higher one goes, the more intelligence and personality enter the picture. Of course one is still subject to the same harsh laws of dismissal if he fails to handle the job properly, but now he is a discredit not only to himself but to the man who hired him. And no supervisor or executive wants to go through the ordeal of firing a man, and then through the humiliation of admitting to his superiors, "I was way off in my judgment of that man. He didn't work out."

The result is that in the majority of cases executives have abdicated their most vital responsibility—the selection of their subordinates—in favor of archaic methods that leave them one vanity-restoring out—"Well he came highly recommended—" or, "He got the highest marks on our intelligence tests."

To put it even more emphatically, the executive knows

little more about the technique of talent buying than the applicant knows about the technique of talent selling, or even that there is a technique. In order to get the best out of a man, you must look for the best that is in him. Success Factor Analysis, the techniques in this book, enables an executive to seek and find the best that is in a man. These techniques also help to adapt men to new technology jobs.

The Great, Unnecessary Sparring Match

As a career development specialist, I have had the opportunity of analyzing thousands of job interviews, both from the executive's side of the desk and the applicant's side. The result has been highly revealing, and in a surprising way.

Contrary to general belief, it is the executive or supervisor with a choice position to fill who is on the most uncomfortable spot. He has to be many things at the same time. He has to play the welcoming host, because the interview takes place in his office, but he can't be sure if he is greeting a guest or meeting an adversary.

He has to be the boss, because he has the power to say "Yes," or "No," fateful words that may dash the applicant's hopes or brighten his whole future, but at the same time he has to subordinate himself to the applicant, thereby encouraging the applicant to talk more freely about himself and supply such other information as the executive needs.

He has to "sell" the position that is open without committing himself to buy the talent that is being offered for sale. By the time he has played a half-dozen roles— in fifteen minutes—host, boss, inquisitor, expositer, encourager, and psychologist, changing hats each time like a quick-change artist, he has had it. And all the time he has had to maintain that air of pleasant good-fellowship demanded of executives while mentally striving to reach that coolly impartial decision that makes or breaks the applicant.

Small wonder that for several years many executives have preferred to let intelligence and aptitude tests weed out their applicants for them. If the results weren't always good, at least it spared them the ordeal of passing judgment on fellow creatures. As one executive, putting in words the thoughts of thousands, explained it to me, "I can buy steel and sell machinery, and drive as sharp a bargain as the next fellow, but buying a man's career—boy, that's something else. I feel like a slave dealer, poking a finger into a man's head to see if there's anything there."

Following the conclusive evidence produced at Columbia University in 1959, that intelligence and aptitude tests as guides to a man's future performance were "little better than guess-work," the whole trend has shifted toward the recognition of a man's achievements as the most reliable guide to selection. This program is already in effect in many leading companies. Achievement analyses select men "in;" old-time methods "weed out" applicants, until the last one remains and is "selected."

In the meantime, with their pet tests discredited, thousands of executives find themselves forced to use the old hiring gate method in filling important jobs, and they don't like it. Whatever the applicant can do to lessen the executive's discomfort, the brighter he makes his own prospects. This you can do by following the procedures detailed in the case history of Tom Strouss, and by keeping the following points in mind:

(1) Few people getting jobs paying more than $8,500 a year are employed at the first interview. So the first must be planned to lead to a second, and because the first is the hardest, it will be well to prepare yourself in advance. Get quiet within yourself; use prayer, and the recognition of God's presence. Let your mind rest for a few moments on the most peaceful scene in nature that you can recall. Boost your self-confidence by recalling your achievements and Dynamic Success Factors. Relate them to the job for which you are applying so they will be fresh in your memory.

Remember that your interviewer is more uncomfortable

than you are, but don't forget he is the boss. Defer to him by returning the command of the interview to him with a question. Be alert in recognizing things that impress him favorably, and try to emphasize them. Toward the end of the interview, if he has not already suggested another executive you might see, ask if he can refer you to one who might be interested.

This is a "memory-fix" technique, linking you in your interviewer's mind with the next executive. Be sure to get the correct spelling of the executive's name and his title, but don't interrupt the interview to jot it down. The receptionist or telephone operator can supply that before you leave the building.

(2) Recognize the responsibility of your interviewer to his company and himself, and don't try to rush him into a quick decision. If a snap-judgment is called for, his safest one is, "No." But do remember to keep your best foot forward, using the technique demonstrated by Strouss, and remain at all times frank and tactful. Also remember this line from Shakespeare: "To thine own self be true and . . . thou canst not then be false to any man." Then, even if he must turn you down, your cooperative attitude will encourage him to suggest other possibilities, or leave the interview open to follow-ups.

(3) The technique of the "open-end interview" has proved invaluable, not only in keeping the door open with your interviewer-of-the-moment, but in frequently leading him to become your "salesman" for other jobs. Let's take the worst possibility—you have been turned down cold. You make a graceful recovery by open-ending your interview in this manner: "Thank you for your time, sir. I do appreciate your consideration, and I want you to know that I realize every applicant cannot fit into your organization. It's your job to tell me that I don't, and I'm grateful for the considerate way you did so. Just the same, in the course of our interview, while you came to know me well enough to realize I won't do here, is it possible that you know me well enough to know where I might fit?"

There is more in the above statement than meets the

eye. The executive has turned you down, but by expressing appreciation of his consideration instead of resentment or disappointment—that would only make him feel guilty and want him to get rid of you the faster—you have demonstrated that you are a nice guy. He doesn't like to reject nice guys.

You have given him psychological relief by easing him out of an uncomfortable situation, moving him to give you what relief he can in return. You have given him that opportunity by asking his advice—always flattering—on a likely place to try next. The chances are two to one that if he knows of such a place or places, he will help you, even going so far as to set up the interviews himself. In one such instance, a client of mine was sent directly to his second interview, where he got the job—at $2000 a year more than the job he had been shooting for.

(4) Follow up your interview with a letter of appreciation. Whether your interviewer has turned you down, or left matters in the air, or referred you to someone else, you have put him through a few uncomfortable minutes. Though there were some good things about the interview—there always are—there were also some adverse, not-so-good, or else you would have been hired. The adverse things are what the interviewer is remembering, if only to justify his action in turning you down or stalling.

Your follow-up letter, which is really a thank-you note few executives get from job seekers, and therefore appreciate all the more, should also contain a condensation of the good things you got out of the interview. Not only does this make him feel good for having done you some good, but your letter, refreshing his memory with the more constructive parts of your conversation, serves to supplant with positive thoughts whatever negative thoughts were raised at your interview. In that mood he may begin to feel that possibly he had been a little hasty in reaching his first judgment.

Here is what we advise our clients on this form of letter-writing: Immediately after your interview, write down a thorough analysis of what was said, both good and bad. Then, since you can't profit from your mistakes, or the bad points, throw them out. Concentrate on what seemed to be of most interest to your interviewer. In the light of hind-sight, you should be able to find several things you said well but which you could have stated better, and you may be able to find one or two strong points that you now recognize to be of special interest to your interviewer that you failed to mention at all. Above all, get down in writing the names, correctly spelled, and titles, of all the executives mentioned during the interview who might have some influence on your future.

Here is one such letter written by a client:

"Dear Sir;

"Thank you for your time and interest Monday afternoon. From what you told me about the company, and from what I have learned since, I am more convinced than ever it is the kind of place where I would be happy to make a contribution. I thought I had prepared myself in advance for the interview, but the inside information you provided during our few minutes together really opened my eyes to the advantages of becoming a member of your team.

"I was particularly attracted by that trouble-shooting job you described. In that respect I would like to add that I get along very well with people in such situations, keeping calm being one of my better attributes. (No. 3 among his Dynamic Success Factors.) You mentioned a Mr. Harold Fisk, your Controller, in connection with that job, and I would certainly like to meet him at any time you could arrange.

"I was also pleased to know that you encourage employees to further their educations (the interviewer's pet project). For your information, I have just completed a university extension course in business management with an A average, and have signed up again for a night course in conversational Spanish.

"The more I find out about your company, the more eager I am to participate in its future growth. Thank you once again. In the meantime, I am looking forward to hearing from you."

He got the job! Yet when he came to me after the interview, he was ready to call it quits. It had been particularly discouraging, the result of a well-meant lead by a contact who hadn't bothered to fill himself in with the details. My client went fully prepared, only to discover he was applying at the right company for the wrong job. "Boy, what a jerk they must think I am at that place now," he said to me.

Maybe so, but his follow-up letter made a friend out of the executive who had been compelled to turn him down, and as a friend he was able to steer my client to the job he might never have heard about.

Circumstances alter factors, but in general you can be sure of a favorable response if your letter shows solid interest in your interviewer and the company he represents, and specifically when the letter reveals that you were attentive enough during the interview to recognize your interviewer's personal fields of interest. By not hitting him again for the job on which he had to turn you down, you have relieved his conscience, and by recalling the name of an associate who might have such a job, you have moved him to become your salesman. And by adding some factors overlooked in the first interview, you have discounted the negative effects produced on that occasion, replacing them with a fresh line of positive thoughts.

(5) In thinking about a step upward, do not confuse the size of the company with the size of the opportunity. It is true that a mediocre man can remain unnoticed in a large company, and even get raises from year to year by virtue of seniority, but the man content with that vegetable type of progress is neither your concern nor mine. It is also true that a well-qualified man can often be recognized quicker in a small concern than in a large one, but that is not too satisfactory, either. Is he really the big frog, he wonders, or is it the pond that's too small? There are some six million companies in the United States, ranging from the crossroads store to General Motors and similar giants. If the jobs were shared equally

amongst them, they would average ten employees each. As it is, a handful of giants employ more than 100,000 persons each, and only some 25,000 companies employ more than 1,000 men and women each. Thus, for all the emphasis on the "corporation man," and the "government or civil service man," it is clear that more people find success in small companies than in large.

I prefer to put it this way. If you want to make a habit of success, you will not be concerned with the protection a large company has to offer the man of mediocre talents, nor will you be content with being the big frog if your pond is a puddle. Static security, big frog or polliwog, can produce only stagnation and rut employment. To take advantage of change and progress, to plan to succeed steadily and excitingly, is not a matter of company size but of personal ambition. To that important subject, the next chapters will be devoted.

chapter 10

WHY, WHEN, AND HOW TO WRITE A RÉSUMÉ

Planning the Campaign

One of the most cherished rituals of employment is the mind-wrenching ceremony called "filling out the application blank." All over the country, in bank after bank of steel files, are millions upon millions of completed application blanks, all looking much alike, and all containing much the same useless information. Of the labors that went into filling them out, of the hopes and ambitions, of the personalities and real achievements of the applicants, only a few hints are revealed. Said one employer of his application file, "The Agony Box. They sweat over filling out the forms, and I sweat over reading them, wondering what the people are really like."

The standard application form of 1974, after 40 years of development, is a statistical clerk's masterpiece—it can screen out just about everybody for any type of work. Everyone with whom I have discussed it—employees, personnel men, agency men, and management—have deplored its short-comings, but they all resort to the same answer: "It's all we've got, and we have to use something."

Theoretically, the application blank is a formalized résumé of the applicant's employment history. It is supposed to show what a man has done, and presumably can do again on the next job. It makes no allowance for how well he did what he did, and provides no assurance that he will do well on the next job. I call it an obituary, because it so successfully buries a man's real values.

To any success-minded man, the whole idea of applying for another job is to further his program for getting ahead. But the application-résumé is designed to disclose only that he is qualified to do much the same work as he has already done.

At the same time it raises a nasty little doubt—maybe he's not so qualified, if he has to hunt for another job. Even an employment history that shows a steady climb from low to high paying positions can raise the same doubts.

All employers are familiar with the glib talker who uses one good job to advance himself to a better two months before his faults catch up to him. Explaining this situation a company president said, "Firing a man is so much trouble he has to make a real mess before we get around to it. We keep hoping he'll go away, and when he gets the drift, he usually does—to a better job. Do we give him a letter of recommendation? Of course. Doesn't everybody? The only letters of recommendation that really mean anything to me are from men I know personally."

If this variety of job jumper has one redeeming value, it's that he proves how easy it is to get a job, even with the wrong talents.

The application-résumé is concerned with the applicant's past. The applicant is concerned with his future. The company is concerned with its future. So why all this concern with what is already obsolete? Even the old saying, "There's no substitute for experience," has lost its significance. Nor is there any validity anymore in the old and desperate complaint, "You can't get a job without experience, and you can't get experience without a job."

Today, with conditions and products changing with bewildering rapidity, too much experience can actually be a handicap. An auditor with 30 years experience in a wholesale house saw his department turned into what he called an "electronic nightmare" that did everything but collect bills from deadbeats. "Thirty years working my way to top of my department," he told me, "and that's the job I got—trying to collect from deadbeats." Fortunately he was an excellent man with tax figures, and is now a successful tax consultant, a job not likely to be taken over by an impersonal machine.

He is but one of the thousands whose jobs and lives are daily being altered in small or drastic ways. As the move toward decentralization by industry and government picks up speed, thousands are faced with the choice of following the job to various sections of the country or remaining where their roots are and hoping to find another job that may or may not have anything to do with past experience. Even in companies that remain firmly rooted, change is the order of the day. Flexibility and adjustability are qualities that are more important in many fields than experience, a word some employers regard as synonymous with "dated," or "rutted," or "not in tune with the times."

The fault lies not with the experience, but in the manner in which it is used. Conditions have changed, products have changed, and so have the methods of making those products, but unchanged remains the thinking surrounding the hiring of the men and women.

This first became a matter of personal concern to me in 1945 when, as a director for the Society for the Advancement of Management (N. Y. Chapter) I was asked to develop a program that would aid our returning veterans in finding jobs. Eighteen executives volunteered to work with me on the placement program, so I began by asking them and others how they had obtained their positions.

That may seem like an obvious beginning, but as it turned out, such a study had never been reported before. Such inquiries had been made previously of personnel men, employment managers, and placement agencies, most of whom were concerned with filling jobs in the lower income brackets. Worse, for my purpose, was the fact that these men were rarely in a position to follow the progress, or the lack thereof, of the men they placed. They knew where the men had come from, but seldom where they were going.

The 18 executives working with me were united in taking an opposite view. Their concern was with what a man could do; not with what he had done. To a man they agreed that they could not get that information from the standard application form. Most of them complained of their inability to get good men through their own personnel offices or through agencies.

And then I got the lead I was looking for. Said one executive, "I can't blame the applicants coming to see me. We've put the emphasis on experience for so long that that's what they've been trained to talk about. I want people with drive and ambition who know where they're going. What I get are people who know where they've been. We need something to shake them up and start them thinking about the future. That's all they've got left to sell, and sure as shooting, that's all we want to buy."

Right then I set out to develop a form of presentation that would show where a man was going, and support it with proof of his ability to get there. It began with the procedures already described in the chapters on Dynamic Success Factors and Functional Self-Analysis and followed through with development of what has since come to be called the Directed Résumé, designed to supplant the obituary-type résumé. In manual form, this work was recommended by the Federal Government for use by returning military officers throughout the country. Its success led in turn to an invitation from the Harvard

Business School for me to serve as a consultant there and add further refinements to the work. Since then, with only such modifications as are needed to meet special requirements, the Directed Résumé has proved its value many thousand times.

Now to get down to cases. The only reason for writing a résumé is to further your progress through moving to another company that offers greater opportunity. That means you have to know where you are going, and have confidence in your ability to get there. Remember the old saw, "If you don't know where you are going, any road will get you there."

Possibly you can arrange your move through contacts and job interviews, but even under these circumstances your interviewer is apt to ask for a résumé, "to pass around to the others who will need to know who you are." That means that your résumé will have to serve as your salesman when you aren't present to talk for yourself. You want your personality in it; not your professional obituary.

By tradition the standard résumé is little more than an elaboration of the standard application form. The unoriginal thinking behind this is based on the supposition that because most companies have come to accept the obituary-type application form, most executives must favor that type of résumé. But as I have already evidenced, most executives are thinking about the future. That is what you must plan to sell.

Some Comparisons

The standard application form starts by asking your name and address. Next follows spaces in which you enter such personal details as date of birth, weight, marital status, etc. A few of the latest forms then ask for the title of the position you are seeking, a somewhat meaningless request since few companies agree on the same duties and responsibilities for the same titles. After that comes the chronological listing of your previous jobs—but in reverse order, with the most recent job first and then on back into history. You are working backwards, while your employer is seeking a man who looks forward.

Nor is that the worst of it. Some of the jobs you must list may have advanced your career and some may have been taken to avert starvation, but on the form, equal emphasis is given to both. You may have excelled on one job and barely held your own on another, but on the form, you appear to be equally good—or bad—on both. It could also be that none of the jobs you held enabled you to use your best abilities, but on the form that fact isn't revealed at all. According to the résumé, you are supposed to be what the jobs made of you; not what you made of the jobs, or what you are able to make of the next one.

It follows then that a standard résumé based on the format of a standard application blank is likely to be a more elaborate presentation of the same weaknesses. About all that can be said for it is that it is easy to write, requiring no imagination and no foresight. Consider, for instance, the chronological résumé of Richard Jones, one of the better examples of the obituary style:

RÉSUMÉ OF RICHARD JONES

1718 E. 191 Street
Brooklyn 19, N. Y.
TEL.: Brook 6-2151

PERSONAL DATA

Age: 34
Marital Status: Married, 2 children
Education: Florida University
Military Service: United States Army—1942–46

BUSINESS EXPERIENCE
Lord and Thompson, Inc.
Present

Merchandising and Sales Promotion

My present responsibilities are

151

in the areas of contests, premiums, incentives, couponing, advertising tie-ins, sampling, direct mail, special audience programs, exhibitions and unmeasured media.

The Universal Metals Company
May 1955 to July 1956

Associate Sales Manager

In this employment capacity, I developed promotions, premium programs, dealer loading merchandising programs in which silver or stainless steel flatware and holloware were the incentive items. The programs developed by me were adopted by many leading national advertisers.

In addition to these creative and sales duties, I was, shortly before my resignation, appointed to handle the liquidation of all excess and inactive inventories of the company and reported directly to the Vice President in Charge of Sales.

Filtration Products, Inc.
November 1951 to May 1955

Advertising and Sales Promotion Manager

In this employment capacity, I was responsible for the administration of an advertising and sales promotion budget of $1,000,000.00 annually, of which approximately $500,000.00 was devoted to national (trade-consumer-industrial) magazine space.

I developed local market advertising (radio-television-newspaper-outdoor) campaign, merchandising and premium programs which were included in the selling programs of 21 petroleum marketers, 6500 automotive parts jobbers and wholesalers, and the Chrysler Corporation, Ford Motor Company, Nash Motors, Packard Motor Car Company, John Deere, The Caterpillar Company, International Harvester Company, Case and Massey Harris tractor companies.

I created-designed-wrote catalogs, bulletins, point-of-sale materials, brochures, direct mail, general sales helps, special literature and display booths.

Enright and Nowey, Inc.
1949–1951

Space Representative-Account Executive

I sold advertising space to national advertisers and developed literature and merchandising packages for these advertisers which were tailored for use in schools, adult education, 4-H activities, home economics shows, home economics school and industry programs.

During this period, I also acted in a consulting capacity to small manufacturers and retailers and prepared copy, rough layouts, promotion literature, publicity and direct mail activity.

Newel Advertising, Inc.
1947–1948

Assistant Space and Time Buyer

Entered training program; ad-

153

vanced through ranks in media detail, media research. Worked on Proctor and Gamble and Nestle Company accounts.

You will note that an 18-year history of Mr. Jones is all there if you can find it, though the names of his employers and dates of employment are given more prominence than what he did. He uses only five words and the dates to cover four years of military service, an experience that must have affected him profoundly. The greatest weakness of all, however, is that Jones has used all that space to tell of what he has sold, and has neglected to mention what he wants to sell. That, of course, is the main fault of the obituary-type résumé, but as an advertising, merchandising, and sales promotion man, one would think Jones would have done something about it.

It could be that he was too close to his own talents to think they needed selling, like the shoemaker whose own children run barefoot, but my experience with too many men indicates otherwise. So fixed in the mind of most is the obituary-type of résumé that they would rather sell themselves short than fail to conform.

Here are the major reasons why the obituary-type résumé should not be used, accepted though it might appear to be:

(1) It fails to inform an employer of your potentialities, forcing him to guess from a reading of your past history what your future value to him might be.

(2) It emphasizes your history, but not what you have learned from it. Almost every résumé lists a number of jobs, and to the employer reading them over, they take on a monotonous sameness. Exposure to experience is not the same as learning from it, and the value of what you learned cannot be estimated by reading that you held—or were stuck with—a certain job for five years.

(3) It emphasizes former employers and dates of employment, an uneasy reminder to your prospective employer that if you could quit them—or get fired—you will quit him—or get fired. It leaves no room to mention

the fact, unless you drag it in by the heels, that you saved or earned uncounted sums for your previous employers and will do better for him.

(4) In stressing your own history, you omit the one factor that is the most vital concern of your prospective employer, and that is his own future and the future of the company that holds his future. Good fellow though he might be, it's not your success he is buying, but his own.

The Functional Résumé

In developing the Functional Résumé for returning veterans, my first concern was with the fixed idea most employers seemed to hold that military experience was of small value in the business world. But for hundreds of thousands of young men, military experience was all they had. I could see employers looking over hundreds of thousands of job applications, all listing Uncle Sam as the employer, and lieutenant as the title of the last job held. Nor would rank offer employers much of a clue, private enterprise having no slots into which corporals, sergeants, lieutenants, majors, colonels, etc., could be automatically fitted. I had to develop a type of résumé that would make individuals of these men instead of dog tags, and so stress their achievements that their future values to an employer would be immediately apparent.

It was no simple résumé, to be filled out in a few minutes, that finally emerged. Nor did I want the boys to get simple jobs in which they might be trapped for weeks, months, or years before they discovered they were getting nowhere. A few hours of work at the start could make the difference between "taking what you can get" and tens of thousands of dollars in habit-forming success.

It began by asking the boys to analyze their achievements to discover their Dynamic Success Factors (the description hadn't yet been coined, but the effect was the same) and followed through with Functional Self-Analysis according to the procedures already described in previous chapters. Now the boys knew what they could do well. The next step was to use this knowledge in setting future goals. More study, of course, of the industries where one could function best, as per Chapter Five, but again far better a few hours spent in a library reading trade journals and company histories than painful time wasted on a dead-end job.

For the thousands interested enough in their success to follow through on the instructions, the results were so spectacular that we were moved to develop the Functional Résumé to assist civilians faced with similar problems. These included war workers whose jobs no longer existed, but who had had no previous experience in other lines of work; men reluctant to pull up family roots when factories began to migrate to the South and West; men who had remained rutted on a single job while their families were growing up, but were now anxious to take "one last flier at success"; and young men with plenty of achievements but no practical experience in business and industry.

Since the Functional Résumé in its present state of development is of more value to you than the one rushed to completion after the war, let's examine the one written recently by Gary Sawyer, a 24-year-old whose practical experience in the eyes of a hard-headed sales manager might be said to be nil:

Age: 24	**GARY D. SAWYER**
Married	Tel: CIrcle 6-8212
Veteran	59 Grace Court
B.A., Yale	Drexel Hill, Pa.

OBJECTIVE	SELLING OR SALES PROMOTIONAL WORK—where use can be made of contact making and persuasive abilities; ingenuity in originating and developing ideas; writing ability; manual skill and understanding of mechanisms—talents that would be useful in demonstrating, trouble shooting, or technical sales.

SALESMANSHIP QUALITIES

Have always been able to meet people easily and have exhibited persuasive abilities on worthwhile subjects. For example:

As a camp counsellor instituted changes in activities of a group of 50 boys that provided more continuous events and more broadening experiences. Doing this involved persuading camp owner and 12 other counsellors that the results justified the extra work involved.

As a community chest solicitor obtained my quota first out of 200 solicitors; then exceeded quota by 85%. . . . Worked up and performed a college radio program that drew favorable response. . . . Originated routines and trained a three-man team of song leaders that appeared before crowds of 70,000.

LEADERSHIP

Through a series of contests and awards, instructing and inspecting, produced a record for camp cleanliness that owner said was the best in 25 years. . . . Directed 50 boys and 15 counsellors in organizing and producing a carnival that was voted best in the history of this event.

MANAGEMENT

Managed camp laundry; had charge of soft drink sales in Navy barracks; coached college soccer team.

IDEAS

Invented a device used by skiers that has been copied and used by professionals; devised a humidifying system for a large residence. Composed words and music for more than fifteen popular and classical songs; planned weekly radio programs; wrote and staged puppet shows.

WRITING   Wrote story for publication throughout all Navy WTS program schools; was in top 5% in short story class, in top quarter of class in theme writing.

MANUAL SKILLS   Rank in 98th percentile on manual dexterity. Designed and built "home workshop projects"; repaired radios and mechanical equipment for puppet shows. Worked on building repairs and construction crew, laid bricks, wooden floors, linoleum; glazed windows.

EMPLOYMENT   Held summer jobs as camp counsellor; laborer on factory maintenance crew, construction and surveying.

First to attract the eye is Gary's name, phone number and address in the upper right hand corner of the page, the traditional space allotted by a newspaper to its most important story. It will also be top-most and instantly readable to anyone thumbing through the job application folder or file cabinet. (Why put your name in the middle or left hand corner of the page where it can be half or completely buried in the file?)

In a less conspicuous but still top-of-the-page or headline spot is his age, marital status, military service, and education.

And then, right into the future with his goal—"OBJECTIVE . . . SELLING OR SALES PROMOTIONAL WORK." No guessing about where he wants to go or his confidence in getting there. With his objective thus firmly planted in his prospective employer's mind, that worthy is bound to read the smaller print to see what the young man can do for him. Thirty-seven words tell him that in seven seconds, and then his eye jumps to the large type in the left margin, again the use of newspaper headline technique. These are the functional words based on previous achievements: "SALESMANSHIP QUALITIES, LEADERSHIP, MANAGEMENT, IDEAS, WRITING, MANUAL SKILLS, EMPLOYMENT." Powerful words that make a powerful first impression.

Then back to "SOME INDICATIONS OF POTENTIAL VALUE." Had Gary written instead, "A RECORD OF PAST EXPERIENCES," the prospective employer would end up by saying, "And not one worth a cent in this high-pressure office." But indications of potential value they certainly were, even to his job as a laborer which indicated he could take it when the going was tough even though he was a Yale man. (Employers from Midwestern and Western colleges are not always impressed by Ivy League men and vice versa.)

In brief, what Gary had done in his résumé was substitute related functions for his lack of practical business experience, and by using the Functional Résumé Form, he had done it so effectively that out of 20 résumés sent out, he received 17 responses. Nine announced with seemingly genuine regret that there were no openings now or in the foreseeable future. One advised him to check back in six months. Seven invited him in for interviews that led to three job offers, the last of which he took at $9,600 a year, somewhat less than the previous two, but with bonus possibilities that he found challenging and enticing.

Now let's consider the following two Functional Résumés written by more experienced men. Had these two written the standard, obituary-type résumés, they would still be in their time-worn ruts. I know, because both had tried the standard résumé often enough to end up with cases of near-permanent despair. See if you can, in reading through Functional Résumés, discover why.

WALTER A. POTTER
5 Johnson Avenue
Baltimore, Maryland

OBJECTIVE   SALES MANAGEMENT

Qualifications   Twelve years' experience as executive

assistant to top policy-making officials along sales, merchandising, and general administrative lines. Successful record in selling and marketing at field and executive levels, familiar with production problems, can work with government officials, act as liaison between departments of company. Made present connection as administrative assistant to national sales manager. Promoted to national assistant sales manager.

AREAS OF EXPERIENCE—SOME ACCOMPLISHMENTS

Management

Guide, train, and develop the sales efforts of national sales organization of fourteen executive salesmen in their relationships with over 2000 distributors and dealers. Also maintain liaison with four company-owned distributor branches insofar as it affects national sales policy.
Staff member of sales policy-making committee; also staff member of advertising, merchandising, and sales promotion committees.

Marketing

Responsible for making field inspections, territorial surveys, and market research, with the view to making recommendations for solution of sales problems. Traveled throughout the United States. Responsible for follow-through on all problems connected with the development, merchandising, and marketing of new lines.

Administration

Responsible for internal sales organization, devising sales records, computing statistics, and sales training. Maintained liaison between departments while introducing new products: have knowledge of buying and production in addition to selling and merchandising.

Previously

Formed and directed new business department for multi-branch New York banking organization to solicit individual, commercial, financial, and industrial accounts. Liaison assistant to president and secretary-treasurer.

National Assistant Sales Manager

Baltimore Paper & Color Corporation, Hagerstown, Md. 1947–Present

Assistant Secretary and Treasurer

Manhattan Trust Company, New York, New York. 1935–1947

Personal Data

Age 35—married—two children. American Institute of Banking and New York University: studied business administration and economics.

FORREST F. WALTERS
Pittsford,
Massachusetts

OBJECTIVE

PRODUCTION AND TROUBLE-SHOOTING ASSISTANT TO PRESIDENT
Experienced in executive and management operations, the development of improved methods to cut costs, training and supervision of employees and foremen, all kinds of investigation and trouble-shooting (in chemical, woodworking, maintenance and construction fields), labor relations and community relations, and plant management.

QUALIFIED BY

More than fifteen years of progressively responsible management and leadership jobs, including Assistant Vice President in Charge of Production for a corporation with sales of $10,000,000, and the elected presidency (three times) of Carpenters' Union. Also, by the self-made man approach to success which includes willingness to learn thoroughly all elements which go towards insuring greatest efficiency and lowest costs.

SOME ACCOMPLISHMENTS

COST CONTROLS
BUDGETING

Saved over $300,000 yearly for one company by analyzing cost elements, developing improved procedures, training supervisors in new methods, installing them, and supervising operations. More than 700 men and women were involved, as well as serious labor problems which were cleared up. . . . Established planned budget exceeding $1,000,000 yearly, and directed expenditures covering labor, materials, repairs, maintenance costs, etc. . . . As Vice President in charge of production with another company, organized, controlled and directed much larger expenditures and purchasing operations.

POLICY-MAKING
ADMINISTRATION
MANAGEMENT
LIAISON

Proved ability to stimulate and maintain friendly relations of all members of management team at joint conferences, frequently in the face of highly controversial issues. Have often been requested to solve management problems requiring objective analysis of antagonistic viewpoints and to reconcile hurt feelings of department heads. With top management, helped develop and execute policy in relation to corporate expansion, location of new plants, selection of key executives and their orientation, coordination of manufacturing with sales potentials, development of new products, planning and organization of new departments and new plants, etc.

PURCHASING

Saved over $20,000 for one company by forward buying of item due to become scarce (its price jumped more than ten times). Purchasing agent for more than 7,500 items. Have always preceded purchases by careful study of specific needs and specific qualities of available supplies. This has made it possible for me to undertake forward buying in many fields, following studies of market and supply conditions and trends, and also to find adequate, lower cost substitutes for many items. Know lumber of different kinds and grades; chemicals; paper; printing; building materials; machinery and maintenance equipment and supplies; woodworking machinery; line-method production equipment and machinery; some plastics; etc.

WOODWORKING PRODUCTION

Thoroughly familiar with all phases of woodworking, from basic carpenter work and housebuilding to fine cabinet work—both on the basis of work with my own hands and as plant manager supervising up to 50 employees producing furniture including logging and sawmill operations.

PRODUCTION & MATERIALS CONTROLS MANUFACTURING METHODS

Boosted output 50% without rise in payroll of 200 personnel: Following study of materials handling and manufacturing methods, developed and installed (through the plant superintendent) improved work and materials flow techniques with the result indicated.

163

Created and installed inventory and materials control systems which maintained supplies at lowest practicable levels, thus insuring minimum capital requirements for non-finished materials, and avoidance of "unexplained" losses. . . . Planned production lines for woodworking, bottling, and other operations, and established production schedules, controls and standards. For these, applied time and motion study techniques, and broad knowledge of machines and mechanical functions.

PLANT BUILDING MANAGEMENT MAINTENANCE

Was in charge of maintenance of all Philadelphia Center Buildings for several years, during which time costs were substantially reduced despite rising prices and wages. Applied scientific management principles, perhaps for the first time on record, to maintenance problems. . . . Directed the largest staff department at Philadelphia Center, handling its problems of policy, personnel recruitment, morale, grievances, and efficiency. . . . Supervised the erection of numerous buildings costing up to $100,000 including residences and factory and office reconstruction. Planned and directed the installation of machinery and equipment, occasionally assisting in design of same. Responsible for plant layout.

NEW PRODUCTS

Helped in the development of several new products, including pre-manufacturing analysis of sales potentials. Hold patents. Have the broad practical design, engineering, and production knowledge which is helpful in the development of new products.

LABOR RELATIONS MORALE BUILDING PERSONNEL TRAINING	Developed merit system, training method for supervisors (conducted these successful classes), and improved training procedures for employees. Built morale with the aid of impartial justice, personal consideration of employees as individuals. Participated in union contract negotiations. Recruited all kinds of personnel, from charwomen to engineers and plant managers, and covering a wide range of union members.
REPORT WRITING TROUBLE- SHOOTING	Prepared numerous reports for top management, principally around cost analysis and cost reduction factors. Many were special trouble-shooting reports made at top management's request. Work has consistently required the kind of patience, perceptiveness, perseverance and analytical abilities that are essential to effective smoothing of troubled waters at management and lower levels.
TRAINING & EDUCATION	Studied intensively in fields which would make me more effective at work. Completed several correspondence courses. Broadly read in many fields. Completed courses offered by professional groups.

The Analysis

For 12 years Walter Potter had served as an executive assistant to the top policy-making officials of his company, the oldest of whom still had ten years to go before retirement. He had had one promotion, from administrative assistant to the national sales manager to national assistant sales manager, an ego-soothing way of saying he still functioned in the same job. His previous 12 years, in which he had risen to Assistant Secretary and Treasurer of one of the many branch offices of a large bank, had been, outside of his salary, largely non-productive because, although he didn't know it then, his Dynamic Success Factors all indicated he belonged in some phase of selling. His lack of a college degree—only two years at NYU and some night courses in banking—had further undermined his confidence. All of his associates, though lacking his ability on which they relied, had college degrees. Only two jobs in 24 years, both of which had led him into dead ends. No wonder he felt discouraged.

Potter was looking only at the stone wall in front of him, not at what his achievements had done for his associates, for the bank, and for the corporation. Once he was able to see the achievements instead of the stone wall, and analyze them in terms of salesmanship where he could function best, the rest was inevitable.

In seven lines, or 30 seconds of reading time, he made clear what he wanted and why he could function profitably in that capacity for a company. Then he drove home such functions as Management, Marketing, and Administration in eye-catching, first-impression words, and documented them with the facts on "AREAS OF EXPERIENCE—SOME ACCOMPLISHMENTS."

He mailed out 30 résumés, and got the response he wanted on his home telephone the next evening. "And to think," he exclaimed to me in describing his new job, "that I had to wait nearly a quarter of a century to realize what it means to enjoy your work!"

The Functional Résumé of Forrest Walters required more planning. He was "more than 50 years old," which he seemed to think was as old as creation. He had not completed his high school education, and though he was well read and had taken several correspondence courses, he felt inferior to college graduates, including his own children, who, incidentally, were more in awe of their father's wisdom than that of any professor they had ever met.

In Walter's appraisal of himself, he was just a "work horse who does what is expected of him." And he was, after more than 30 years with the same company, tired of being a horse. (In his résumé, you will note, we ignored his first years of working his way up to management level, and stated honestly, "More than fifteen years of progressively responsible management and leadership jobs." It was this we had to sell, and not the years it took him to get there, a fact all oldsters who think they have nothing left to sell should put foremost in their minds. This is the same policy in selling yourself to your new employer that the salesman uses in introducing the new model car; it may be only a slightly revised version of last year's model, but by the time he gets through stressing the new features, you are left with the impression that not an old feature remains.

Once Walters had analyzed his achievements, he no longer saw himself as a man whose 30-year career was on the down-grade to retirement. Maybe his present company thought of him as "the old reliable workhorse," but he could see his Dynamic Success Factors opening up a whole new future. He was "thinking rich" again, and feeling all the younger for it. On the strength of this new surge of confidence, he sat down to dream up "the ideal job" that would use his success factors to best advantage.

Note that he did not think of a specific job, and then try to fit his success factors to it; he let his success factors create a "dream job," and then set out to find if such a job actually existed or could be conjured up. "As long as I'm not going to get the job anyway," he said to me, "I might as well not get the best."

Well, he was thinking of the best, even if in negative terms. And he was thinking creatively. One of the most overlooked points in résumé writing is that in today's rapidly changing world, opportunities are opening so fast that not even the employers are always aware of their imminence. Then along comes the right résumé, and the employer finds himself saying with astonishment and relief, "Boy, that's the kind of a man we've been needing for a long time."

That is exactly what happened in Walters' case. A harassed executive vice president, too busy to realize he was working himself to death, saw in Walters' résumé the solution of all his problems. Some of his problems, as Walters told me later, the executive didn't know he had.

"The whole thing was mixed up," Walters said. "The company had picked up six new lines in the last two years, including prefabricated houses and aluminum boats. The whole plant had been modernized by an engineering consultant firm, but no one had overhauled management. One senior V.P. was still in charge of storm windows, sashes and doors and could play golf every day. A junior V.P. was in charge of what they called the 'toy department,' turning out about a million dollars' worth of boats a year, and knocking himself cold. The hardest trouble-shooting job I had was convincing old-time management that boats weren't toys anymore, and that the management load had to be more evenly distributed. The senior V.P. doesn't like me for busting up his golf game, but as long as my boss and the junior V.P. are getting in a little time for fishing these days, I don't have to worry."

And Walters, having the time of his life, was getting in a little fishing, too, and one of the items he fished up was a doubling of his previous salary.

The Directed Résumé

The Directed Résumé is a development of the Functional Résumé, intended for use by men whose employment history includes several jobs. Its preparation requires the same selective thinking demanded by the Functional Résumé because it must represent your future as you see it—and want your employer to see it—and not serve as an obituary of your professional past.

Whether you like it or not, and no one does, the fact remains that the suspicion of job-jumping hangs over the man who has moved more than five times during his first ten years of employment. And the belief exists, especially among younger employers, that any man who has not found his niche by the age of (30) is never going to find it. In the first instance, there are just enough job-jumpers to provide some foundation for the suspicion, and in the second instance, there are just enough men over (30) so regimented in their thinking that any change, even for the better, is intolerable. Such being the case, the conditions exist and must be faced.

Thus the purpose of the Directed Résumé is not to list your experiences like so many groceries, but to direct them at the job you are after, as though you had dedicated your professional life to preparing yourself for this ultimate position. No repetition of experiences, but an accumulation of them, all adding up to a potential of enormous value to your next employer.

Let's consider first the standard résumé of Warren Arthur that drew dusty answers in response to 50 mailings. Then compare it with the Directed Résumé that follows.

RÉSUMÉ

WARREN ARTHUR
419 Cedarlane Avenue
Allenport, L. I., N. Y.   Telephone—JOhnson 4-2199

Born—Asbury, New Jersey—May 3, 1915
Marital Status—Married—four children
Health—Excellent—Height 6'1"—Weight 197
Education—Clairview Academy—10 years
            Somernet Hills Preparatory School—2 years
            New York College—Industrial Relations &
            Personnel Courses

WORK HISTORY

March 1951 to Present
DIRECTOR OF PERSONNEL—Graves Electronics
                            Corporation, Newroads,
                            L. I., N. Y.
Manufacturer of electronic computers employing over 2400 employees. Supervise all Personnel operations which include the following:
Employment Manager, Training Supervisor, Employee Relations Manager, Editor and staff of company newspaper (issued monthly), Wage and Salary Administrator,

Security Officer and Security Force of approximately forty guards, Insurance Supervisor, Medical Department of four nurses and physician, and Personnel Department Clerical Staff. Responsible also for the plant cafeteria's operation.

(It is interesting to note that management has been successful in keeping the plant non-union through the entire history of its operation.)

August 1945 to March 1951

PERSONNEL MANAGER—Blueright, Inc., Brooklyn, N. Y.

In addition to employment duties and other personnel functions, I was the company representative at the weekly grievance committee meetings of the IAM, Carpenters and Joiners Union, and Local 3 of the Electricians Union. I also was a member of the company negotiation team.

Prior to above

MERIT RATING SUPERVISOR—Superrise Company, Briarcliff, N. Y.

PERSONNEL MANAGER—Aviation Products, Whitestone, N. Y.

ASS'T PERSONNEL DIRECTOR—Airlift Producers, Inc.

EMPLOYMENT INTERVIEWER—The Ajax Corporation

Personnel background covers a total of fifteen years.

MEMBER: New York Personnel Management Association

The Long Island Personnel Directors' Association

WARREN ARTHUR
TEL: JOhnson 4-2199
419 Cedarlane Avenue
Allenport, L. I., N. Y.

SCIENTIST RECRUITER and INDUSTRIAL RELATIONS—PERSONNEL EXECUTIVE: Experienced in both union contract negotiations and non-union manufacturing operations—with medium-sized companies employing between 500 and 2400 personnel of all kinds—in the electronics, aircraft parts, electro-mechanical components and rubber-products industries. Twelve years of reporting to

170

the President and working with him on the policy committee; interviewed (and recruited) all applicants for key professional and managerial positions; initiated and conducted training and development programs (also supervised training director); established new safety program (which reduced insurance costs); directed employee publications program; maintained community and inter-industry relations; and otherwise established and directed industrial relations and personnel programs—from the point of beginning one.

6'1", 197 lbs., age 43, excellent health, married, 4 children, will relocate.

DIRECTOR OF PERSONNEL, manufacturer of missile and electronic equipment components—Graves Electronics Corporation, 1951–1958. Directed expansion of personnel from 800 to over 2400, and contraction due to military cutbacks and economic changes. Supervised all phases, including supervisor training, wage and salary administration, security, medical department, cafeteria, monthly publication, etc. Very effective in communications and human relations (guided policy and activities which resulted in 3:1 employee vote to remain independent of union affiliation). Reported to the President.

INDUSTRIAL RELATIONS DIRECTOR (actual title, Personnel Manager), with manufacturer of rubber products used in the construction industry; 900 employees, 3 IAM unions—Blueright, Inc., 1945–1951. Maintained effective relationships with union representatives, and kept formal grievances to a minimum; with production Vice President and Labor Attorney, negotiated union contracts. Responsibilities included all recruiting, plant feeding, supervisor training, editing employee publication, department administration. Reported to President.

MERIT RATING SUPERVISOR—Supervise Company, Briarcliff, N. Y. (4,500 emp.)

PERSONNEL MANAGER—Aviation Products, Whitestone, N. Y. (1,200 emp.)

ASS'T PERSONNEL DIRECTOR—Airlift Products, Inc., (700 emp.)

EMPLOYMENT INTERVIEWER—Ajax Corporation (1,200 emp.)

MEMBER: New York Personnel Management Association

It should be obvious from the analyses of the Functional Résumés of Sawyer, Potter, and Walters why Warren Arthur got his job within two weeks after sending his Directed Résumé to ten carefully selected companies.

Now consider the résumés of Jack Minus, a young man of 33 who had really floundered around from taxi cab companies and retail stores to wholesale houses and a motion picture company. He was not a job-jumper. With each move he had hoped to better himself, in a disorganized sort of way. The disorganization is evident in his standard résumé which neglects to mention where he wants to go and lumps his colorful experiences with a taxi cab company, dress maker, etc., under the dull heading of "Private Industry: Bookkeeper; . . ." But see how it all adds up in support of his objective in the Directed Résumé.

JACK MINUS
1105 Newark Avenue
Bronx 17, New York
GRand 2-1965

Personal History: Born August, 1924, NYC
       Married: Two dependents
       Weight 144, height 5'7½"

Business Experience: January 1954 to June 1956

Currently employed by a medium size Certified Public Accounting firm. This organization has a diversified clientele of manufacturers, retail stores, insurance companies, and automotive fleets. My responsibilities include work of original entry; preparation of financial statements; tax returns and audits both supervised and unsupervised. As an outgrowth of my work, I have developed a deep interest in dealing with people and seeking a fresh approach to systems and procedures whenever a situation may warrant change.

Aaron Jones, C.P.A. September 1952 to December 1953
New York, N. Y.

A. R. Mour & Co. August 1951 to June 1952
New York, N. Y.

My duties with the above mentioned firms consisted of footing books of original entry; computing sales invoices and their sequence of numbers; bank reconciliations, confirmation of accounts receivable and numerous other procedures of a junior accountant.

Private Industry: February 1948 to August 1951
   Bookkeeper; accounts receivable clerk; inventory clerk; and general office procedures.

Education:

Graduated 1947—Roosevelt High School, New York, N. Y.

Graduated 1954—New Columbia University, Brooklyn, N. Y.
                        Bachelor of Science in Accounting
                        Evening Session

Military Service:
   Radio Technician in the United States Air Force. Honorably discharged.

                        JACK MINUS
                        GRand 2-1965
                        1105 Newark Avenue
                        Bronx 17, New York

OBJECTIVE   ASSISTANT OFFICE MANAGER, with responsibilities which would include analysis and development of systems and procedures, work on internal auditing and accounting supervision, related problem solving, and working with and supervising office personnel on associated details.

SUMMARY OF   More than eight years of diversified
BACKGROUND   auditing and accounting experience in supervisory office position, and with public accounting firms (B.S. Accounting). As General Accountant and Assistant to Chief Auditor (currently), introduced revised forms which gave more complete data and increased paper handling efficiency. . . . As General Accountant, worked on budget analysis, monthly and progressive statements and supporting

173

schedules, and special assignments for Auditor. . . . As Public Accountant, served as semi-senior and junior; responsible for unsupervised audits of small firms, and supervised audits with larger companies; prepared financial statements and tax returns; developed and installed complete simple bookkeeping systems.

PERSONAL DATA

Age 33, 5'7½", 145 lbs., good health, married, one child. B.S. Accounting, New Columbia University.

VARIETY OF EXPERIENCE

Now with producer of movie films; previously, accounting and auditing work with such concerns as insurance broker, wholesale drug concern, wholesale distributor, dress manufacturer, taxicab company, bakeries, retail stores, etc.

EMPLOYMENT HISTORY

General Accountant and Assistant to Chief Auditor—MGM Laboratories, Inc. (1956–now). Developed report to improve office work flow, simplify and improve the efficiency of office operations, conducted and supervised audits, analyzed budgets, helped coordinate data from different departments, worked with clerical and supervisory personnel from several departments.

Semi-senior and Junior Accountant (1951–1956). Duties included general tax, auditing, accounting and bookkeeping work, as well as development of systems improvements, installation of systems, training of bookkeeping and related clerical personnel, and some advisement with small company principals. The CPA firms were: B. Winickot & Co. (1954–56); Aaron

Jones (1952–53); and A. R. Mour & Co. (1951–52).

PREFERENCE   Would prefer working in an organization under a progressive office manager, Controller or Assistant Treasurer.

Some Pointers

(1) Describe the position you want—your objective—but do so in terms of your ability to function well in it. In these changing times, that job might have been made obsolete overnight, but your abilities are not subject to obsolescence. In both the Functional and Directed Résumés you are stressing your values, and something of value is what an employer wants, and can use.

(2) If you are young and eager, but relatively inexperienced businesswise, stress youth and ambition, and build up your achievements in related functions. If you are rich in age and experience, select those experiences that can be directed at the job you want, and leave your age out of it, or drop it in casually as a support for your mature judgment.

(3) Don't hesitate to conjure up the "ideal" or "dream" job. Simply because you have never heard of such a position doesn't mean that it might not be the answer to a harassed executive's prayer. Many a job's requirements have been altered to take advantage of an applicant's superior values.

(4) Don't ever believe that an employer really knows what he wants, much though that belief has been foisted about. He may think he knows, as he may think he knows his wife will like perfume for an anniversary present, but you can be sure that if he is offered something more attractive while in a buying mood, he'll take it. What he buys is more influenced by what he can get than what he thinks he wants.

(5) Never overlook the assets of military experience. Though few executives like to admit it, they are now

aware of the fact that men with military experience often execute orders better than those without it. To this can be added the sneaky suspicion, "How come you dodged military service, or weren't fit for it?" (Those who for a variety of legitimate reasons were never privileged to serve, please note, and prepare forthright answers to an unavoidable question.)

But in relating your military achievements to the job you are after, select only those that can be directly applied, and then describe them in *civilianese*. Capturing a machine gun nest occupied by 20 North Koreans is certainly an heroic achievement, but if the job you are after is in textile design, the mention of such heroism could condemn you as a swashbuckling adventurer who would never do in making designs of colored threads. And if you were in command of large numbers of men, don't use that fact to snow an employer who may head up a small but select group. He may think you are too big for the job.

(6) In presenting your achievements or business background, select those facts which support most strongly your bid for the job you are after. When you stated your objective, and backed it with a few lines describing your abilities—what we call a "frame of reference paragraph" —you were saying in effect, "This is how I would like you to think about me." If you stated that your objective was office manager, for instance, you are asking him to think of you as a manager. If you don't substantiate, or "flesh out," this skeleton outline with real or related experience, you have seriously weakened your case.

(7) If you have had several jobs, examine them to see if their contributions to your experience can be summarized in a single paragraph. "Sales work with department store, grocery, filling station and all-night restaurant," is a far stronger way of presenting yourself as a salesman than would be a listing of four separate jobs.

Look at it this way: The listing of four "little jobs" creates in your prospective employer the psychological impression that you are a "little job" man; the grouping of them in a single paragraph creates the impression that you have accumulated an interesting, and hence valuable, series of experiences. Many an employer was himself a clerk, counterman or grease monkey, and can appreciate your use of "sales work" as a related description of the job. That in itself is a demonstration of good salesmanship.

(8) Remember that a "little job" is a matter of degree. No job is small to the man who is proud of it, and no job is big to the man who wants something bigger. Apply Point 7 to your résumé, no matter how high the goal you are shooting at.

(9) Humanize your prospective employer. It is true that a favorable decision from him can have a profound effect on your future, but that doesn't make him a demigod. While you are working over your own résumé, you might pause to wonder how many he sweated over before he got to where he is. Unless you are moving into a business handed down from father to son, you are directing your résumé at a success-minded man like yourself who is apt to forget where he came from. Such being the case, you might pause to wonder, also, about what you'll think of a résumé like yours when you succeed your prospective employer in his present post. That puts you in the position of selling yourself on your own future, and if you're sold, you have complied with the first rule of salesmanship—"The best salesman is a satisfied customer."

chapter **11**

HOW TO GET YOUR RAISE—
AND PROMOTION

How to Know When a Raise Is a Raise

Within the last 50 years a man's productivity, and hence earning power, has increased so enormously that salary raises are handed out with what seems to be automatic regularity for a variety of reasons. Of course labor and management see nothing automatic about the process, leaders of the former trying to "better conditions for the workingman" and leaders of the latter trying to "hold the price line to stop inflation." I don't intend to enter that debate. Some of the highest-priced brains in the world have been working on that problem from both sides of the fence, and the fence seems to be just as strong as ever. In fact, when our future generation arrives to colonize Venus, I am sure it will take up the labor-management problem at about where it was when the first man went to work for another.

My concern is exclusively with the individual who wants to make a habit of success. He faces some new problems seldom studied, and then only rarely understood. Management has its problems, and labor has its problems, and if the individual caught in between has his problems, well—that's his own lookout, or so goes the general line of thinking.

Yet the success-minded individualist is the backbone of our creative civilization. And today, faced with periodic pay raises to meet increased costs of living, faced with pay raises based on seniority, faced with pension plans, and Social Security, and medical benefits, he is finding it far easier to "take what is coming to him" than exercise his God-given talents. This can be boiled down to the fact that the biggest obstacle in the course to success today is the comfort we can heap on mediocrity.

I do not believe that a salary adjusted to meet an increased cost of living is a raise. I do not believe a salary increase based on length of service is a raise. And I must deplore the continued employment of men on jobs made obsolete by technical advances—featherbedding is the usual term—for two reasons: In the first place a man not carrying his own weight reduces the productivity average of his associates, and in the second place, the featherbedder suffers enormously in damaged morale, knowing that he is drawing good wages for a job that serves no useful purpose.

What does this mean to you? Much! When raises are handed out at periodic intervals to meet increased living costs or the demands of seniority, the man whose contributions to increased efficiency entitle him to a raise is more apt to be reminded of the raises he has already received than the raise he *deserves*. Where featherbedding is practised, his increased productivity is needed to meet the drain of men who produce nothing. And while it is true that only mediocrity is incouraged when people can get pay raises by virtue of increased living costs or seniority, regardless of initiative, little is being done to alleviate this situation. As a matter of fact, the man whose superior talents entitle him to a raise is too often regarded as a problem. If he is granted the raise because he has earned it, all of his associates will want raises because group raises have become a fixture in group thinking, and no employer likes to choose between a group raise or a discontented crew.

The net, and much more serious result, is that extra effort and the employment of superior talent tends to be discouraged. As "group-thinking" has it, there is just so much money in the pot to be parceled out in raises. If one man gets an individual raise, there is that much less when the time comes to "slice the turkey." No one knows this better than management, and to keep the peace, they would rather have one somewhat discouraged top performer on their hands than a score or more of his discontented associates demanding to know why the company couldn't afford to give them raises if it could give him one.

Most books and articles on how to become successful are helpful in telling you what to do while omitting to tell you what you are up against. The advice may be good, but it loses its effectiveness if you are still working in the dark. Labor has developed some techniques to win increased salaries for all. Management has developed some techniques to protect itself from the more exorbitant features of increased salary demands. Abuses of these techniques exist on both sides, and crushed in the middle is the ambitious individual who would proceed on personal merit.

Your top executive in management was such a climber. Your top labor leader was such a climber. Both climbed to the top by asserting their individualism and making the most of their talents, and yet both seem to be united in reducing individualists to conformists who can be more easily regimented.

Management Wage Policy

Maybe they figure that if an individual has the energy and ambition, he will find his way to the top as they did, but I would put it this way: So swiftly have conditions changed in the last 15 years that if the men now occupying top positions in labor and management had to start over, many of them would find themselves regimented in subordinate positions by the very practices they helped originate. Let me list a few of these practices so you will recognize them if you meet them.

First would be the "annual review," a procedure through which management scrutinizes the payroll once a year and reevaluates salaries, usually upping them. Theoretically, you are thus assured that your salary will be examined at annual intervals and your contributions to company efficiency will then be recognized and rewarded.

Actually the procedure is a handy way of avoiding the consideration of raises during the other months of the year, a special hardship on men of ability who progress faster and contribute more than their associates. It is also hard on the new employee hired just after the annual review and whose talents might have to wait another twenty months for recognition. And while management tries to establish the fact that raises are for those who earned them, they are usually so widely distributed to keep everyone happy that little or no difference is drawn between the bench warmers and the hard players. The unhappy result—the incentive to achieve excellence is lowered, and the hard players soon learn to "join the team" on the bench.

Then there is the time-honored practice of "Management by Exception," advocated by most of the standard books on business management. The business graph on the wall, made famous by cartoonists, is a part of it. The graph is supposed to indicate the course of sales or production, usually hopefully upward, and any deviation from the chart up or down—any exception—is thereby instantly revealed, and instantly acted upon. In the same way, records are kept of what each employee is expected to produce, and the alert supervisor is supposed to detect immediately any exception to the norm.

Theoretically, the supervisor should be as happy to detect a superior performance as a sales manager would be to detect signs of a boom, but it does not work out that way in the majority of instances. Most supervisors think of themselves as "fire fighters" or "trouble shooters," and in that frame of mind they are alert to detect any signs of inefficiency that threaten to give their department a bad name. The lazy or inefficient worker is soon dealt with. The average worker who does what is expected of him is considered to be "no problem" by the supervisor. The gifted, or "exceptional" man should be, according to the rules, as much of a problem as the below-par man. He should be recommended for promotion, and another man brought in to take his place, all of which involves a lot of paper work and training that the supervisor would rather not face.

Far better, in his opinion, to have a superior man around to help out in emergencies than to promote him and face breaking in another man who might be of no value whatever. Thus while "Management by Exception" does serve to weed out the incompetents, it usually continues to breed mediocrity by failing to give recognition to merit.

Another hurdle in the path of personal progress is the established belief in many companies that the cost of promoting a man and "breaking him in on the new job" exceeds his worth for months or even years. At one time it was believed that a graduate engineer had to spend two years in the field before he earned back his first year's salary. I know it is often the case that management spends thousands of dollars over and beyond a man's salary in breaking him in on a new job, but I consider this extravagance a case of pure shortsightedness on the part of management.

Either it failed to prepare a man properly for his new responsibilities, or it did not know how to select the right man for the job. In either case, management deserves to pay extra for its deficiencies. But while I can't feel sorry for management under such circumstances, I do regret that it has made management, on the whole, hesitant about handing out raises and promotions as rapidly as it should for its own good.

What these practices all add up to is a serious case

of management inertia. It believes that if it gives a raise to one, it must give corresponding raises to others, and it is cheaper to let one man suffer than raise the whole crew. It believes that if a superior man is doing a good job, he is usually no problem and so can be left where he is. It believes that promoting a man entails all sorts of training expenses and uncertainties, not to mention the paper work, so why take the risk that he will flop? Laboring under this negative attitude, it is loathe to move at all.

When and How to Get a Raise

Well, it is the job of placement counsellors to find the problems so we can provide solutions, and this we have done. Now I'm going to give you the techniques for getting your raise in spite of the aforementioned obstacles, techniques that have worked consistently for thousands of people in all kinds of work.

I'll summarize the four steps first, and then supply the details:

(1) Be sure you have earned your raise.
(2) Be sure your supervisor knows you have earned it.
(3) Be sure he knows that you know you have earned it.
(4) Be sure he knows you know he knows.

That's all there is to it. Brief enough to be easily memorized, and well worth it.

The first thing the above summary does is return the problem of getting a raise to the one man who wants it—you. No one else wants problems, and least of all do they want someone else's. Are you fully informed on what you have been doing, and how well you have been doing it? The great probability is that if you have been performing with above-average ability, you have been placed in a "let well enough alone" category, and so have heard few words of praise or condemnation on which to base an opinion. Until you make your own appraisal of your situation, you won't know where you stand.

Well, "Management by Exception" is not a procedure limited to management. You have the same prerogative. Keep a written record of what is expected of your job, and especially keep track whenever your performance has exceeded that which was expected of you. In that way you can document your claim to having earned a raise. The next, and more diplomatic step, is to let your supervisor know you have earned it.

I was fortunate enough to learn about this step on my first job by doing it all wrong. Even then, at 19, I was opposed to hard work, having some elementary idea that jobs should supply a lot of enjoyment and money. Part of my work was to check billings to customers. Another part was to check with the warehouse foreman on the delivery of materials, and a third part was to accept telephoned orders from customers. That last part was complicated by the fact that before I could assure the customer his order would be filled, I had to shout back to the foreman to find out if the merchandise was in stock.

I followed procedure for a month or so to solidify my hold on the job, and then I began to hunt for easier ways out. Today we would say I began "seeking ways to increase efficiency." I began keeping track of incoming stock and out-going orders on opposite pages of a cheap notebook. It was not an original system but, never having studied bookkeeping, it was original with me, and I was proud of it. Within a month I knew as much about the merchandise we had left in the warehouse as did the foreman, and no longer had to shout back to him to ask if such-and-such an item was in stock. I was saving both of us a lot of work, but that is not the recognition I got.

I was in trouble. I had gone over the foreman's head. By filling orders without consulting him first, I had left him uninformed of what was going on in his own domain, and that was bad. True, he could see from my record what was coming in and going out, but he didn't want to have to "consult with a kid" to discover what was going on. He reported me to the owner of the wholesale house, claiming that I was a spy keeping secret records of the company's business, "For no good purpose, I'll warrant."

The next I knew, the boss came storming in and snatched my notebook right out from under my hand as I was making an entry, leaving a large scrawl across the page. "Now I'll find out what kind of a trick you are up to," he shouted, and stormed out. I sat out the rest of the day, knowing I was fired, but afraid to leave for fear it would look like some kind of an admission of guilt. Shortly before quitting time the boss returned, this time in a calmer mood.

"You had better explain this to me," he said. "It looks like an auditing system I'm interested in, but the way you have it here, I can't make it out."

We were able to get together then, and when he discovered my system was not a nefarious plot to sell his business secrets to some rival concern, we were able to talk until way into the night.

In the end he said, "All right, I'm going to approve of your system, and make it a part of our company records. But never take off on your own again without consulting me first. You made an enemy of the foreman, one of my oldest employees, but I think I can square that when he gets the orders from me instead of you. Just stay out of his way for a while, and he'll calm down. And if you happen to get a raise in your salary, don't say anything about that, either."

The above anecdote illustrates another of the big obstacles in your way to a salary increase—the ignorance of your immediate superior of what you are doing. You may think you are doing him a favor and saving him a lot of unnecessary work, as I did, but unless he knows that that is what you are doing, his reaction is apt to be quite hostile.

When you take your talents for granted, you assume that they are equally obvious to others, and this is rarely the case. The foreman didn't know if I was saving him work, or trying to beat him out of his job. Had I informed him about my plans—and the best way to do that is through asking his advice about them—I would have won him over as a friend and an ally. As it was, it was some weeks before I could convince him I was not plotting to undermine his job.

Nevertheless, I had done something that had improved the stock-handling procedure of the company. My foreman had brought my work to the attention of the owner—not, I'll admit to get me a raise but to expose my "plot"—and when my contribution proved to be of value, I got my raise.

Of course there was a lot of "luck" connected with my first raise. I really didn't know I had done anything special. I thought of my inventory system as something developed "in the line of duty," and would have thought myself presumptuous had I called it to the attention of the owner. Not until later, when I began to hunger for a second raise, did I realize that Lady Luck was not going to come around with raises as often as I might like.

It was then that I sat down to write a list of reasons, based on my contributions to the company, as to why I had earned another raise. When my list also included the fact that my foreman had handled some $50,000 more in merchandise than he had during the previous year, and at no additional cost to the company, he was quite willing to pass the information on to the owner. We both got raises.

Ever since then I have been a strong advocate of the four steps previously enumerated. Before you can ask for a raise, you've got to know you have earned one, and this you can learn only by keeping written records. In today's business world, few are the supervisors who will tell you when your performance is above average and hence deserving of a raise. At best they'll let you know you are doing as well as is expected of you, and hope you'll let it go at that. Most people will. When all the emphasis is on "making good" instead of "doing better," the majority of men are more concerned about making a mistake—slipping below what is expected of them—than they are with special contributions. That still doesn't stop the contributions from being raise-worthy and praise-worthy if they are recognized and written down.

Two important things happen when you begin to keep a record of your above-par work. First, you are "thinking rich" when you are looking for your highest values instead of your "get along" values. And second, when you are conscious of your written progress report, and several days pass in which you have nothing significant to record, you will begin looking over the job to see what more contributions you can make, if only to add something to the report. One of my clients became so obsessed with adding one daily contribution to his "work diary" that he was actually astonished when he found himself marked for a raise.

How Much of a Raise Do You Want?

I've heard men say, "I really don't care how big the raise is, just so I get some recognition for my work." What hurts me is that they are sincere when they say it. They are more starved for the pat on the back that the raise symbolizes than they are for the money. My own idea is that if a man is worthy of a raise, the raise should be worthy of him.

Here you must keep in mind the fact that even the fairest of employers must profit from your enterprise. If you work out a program that saves $5,000 a year for the company, and are rewarded with a $5,000 a year raise, you haven't saved the company a cent. Or let's say you work out a routing that saves the company a thousand dollars on a costly freight shipment, and are rewarded with a $50-a-month raise. Unless you can come up with more cost-reducing procedures, and soon, your raise will devour your original savings, and the company will begin looking at you with a yellowed eye.

In the former instance, where the savings effected for the company continue year after year, you have produced the equivalent of a patented product that returns an

annual profit of $5,000. A proportionate increase in salary
is indicated plus, possibly, a bonus for the creation of
the original cost-reducing plan. In the case of the once-
in-a-blue-moon savings on a big freight shipment, I would
consider a one-shot bonus of one or two hundred dollars
as a fair reward for a one-shot accomplishment.

The important point is that in both cases you have
to keep your own records to prove that the company
has benefited, or you cannot expect to be rewarded *in
proportion* to your contributions. Again it's a case of,
"If you don't know you've done anything special, why
should anyone else?"

What kind of a record should you keep? The best
place to start is with the date of your employment, or,
if you have had raises since then, the date of your last
raise. Just what were you doing then? Below are four
forms to assist you. Use a separate sheet of paper for
each, starting out with the questions as listed and following through on the rest of the page with the details.

Salary Increase Form No. 1

What was the date of your last salary increase?.............
How much was your raise? $...................................per
(Week, month or year)
List here your duties and responsibilities just after you
had the raise:

Form No. 2 is intended to show where possible the
difference between your job before the raise and your
job after the raise.

Salary Increase Form No. 2

a. What were your job duties and responsibilities before
the date given on Form No. 1?
b. Were there any special reasons for your being given
the raise? If so, describe briefly.

Form No. 3 relates to your contributions since your last raise. It sometimes happens that increases are given in anticipation of increased results; that is why your answers on Form No. 3 may need to be considered along with your answers to Item b. in Form No. 2. In the great majority of cases, however, contributions or improvements are followed by a raise.

Salary Increase Form No. 3

Describe your contributions (alone, or in association with others—say which) since the date of your last raise.

Form No. 4 is a record of your present duties and responsibilities. This enables you to compare the changes in these which may have taken place since your last raise.

Salary Increase Form No. 4

What are your duties and responsibilities, now?

In completing the above forms, each must be considered as independent of the others. Do *not* refer to the answers in one while filling out the next. Not until all have been completed should they be compared, and then the comparisons should answer the following questions:

(1) Why did you receive your last raise?

(2) What have you done since that makes you feel you deserve a raise now?

(3) Why should your supervisor and other executives share your conviction that you have earned a raise?

With this information you are now prepared to take Step Two. You know you have earned your raise. Now make sure your supervisor knows you have earned it. This is sometimes difficult, and almost always delicate, but as always, honesty is the best policy. Here is how George Wiley met the situation:

George had made the jump from a small chemical company to the giant chemical concern of Dulac, Inc., with the vague idea that if he jumped from a little outfit to a big one his success would be scaled accordingly. Instead, after two-and-a-half years as a Senior Engineer and assistant to the Division Manager, he was still just that at no increase in salary. The Division Manager, within two years of retirement, had come to depend upon George, and was in no hurry to see him promoted. Quite congenially he agreed that George was deserving of a raise, but, regretfully, he had to state that George was already in the top salary bracket when one considered his age, length of time with the company, and his Senior Engineer title.

George suggested a transfer to another department and a new title that warranted an increase in salary. The old gent agreed that this was the solution, but he never found time to act on it. It was the old Army game. George could not get a promotion until his superior approved it, and the superior wasn't going to approve an act that was tantamount to severing his professional right arm.

When George came to me, he was ready to quit. Prices were rising, he said, and his salary wasn't. His wife was bitter because they couldn't afford to join the country club that was a status symbol separating the successes from the failures. George didn't care about the club, but he did object to the fact that many of his college fraternity brothers of less talent were ahead of him in prestige and salary.

I knew Dulac was a good company, and after I had heard all of George's story, I was convinced he could find his success there if he could get himself out of the trap into which he had jumped. If only he had taken the time to analyze the job before jumping—! But jumped he had, and trapped he was. Nevertheless, business traditions are made by men, and what men have made, men can change. That has to be true, or there would be no change, no progress, at all.

Remember that if you run into a stone wall. As the whole world changes from hour to hour, so must change the rules that have nothing to support them but tradition. Any time you hear the words, "It's a rule around here not to—" or "It is company policy to—" you know something is in need of up-dating, and you might get an additional raise for doing so.

I had George go through all the procedures described in this book, from the analysis of his achievements and Functional Self-Analysis to the completion of the four forms prescribed in this chapter. Amazingly, for a man of his education and experience, he knew very little about Dulac, Inc., beyond the limits of the job that had absorbed all of his time.

He knew, of course, that the company was expanding rapidly in the fields of chemicals, plastics, paints, and fertilizers, but not until he had completed his research in company history and had "functionalized" several jobs in various departments did he realize what a wide range of opportunities it offered a man of his ability. And more surprisingly, not until he had "functionalized" his own job in terms of corresponding jobs did he realize that he was actually functioning as a Division Administrator, a job about three levels above that of Senior Engineer. His crusty old boss, coasting on the downgrade to retirement, had eased out of most of his responsibilities and was "letting George do it" with a vengeance.

We agreed that George's boss was not going to be very cooperative in advancing George's cause. At the same time, "lines of command" were firmly established at Dulac, and to go over a supervisor's head was a breach of etiquette that could lead to serious trouble. That meant we had to go over the man's head without appearing to do so.

I suggested that George develop a forecast of his career for the next twelve months, documenting it in the same way the company documented its own annual forecast. He began with a summary of the talents and values he had brought to the company at the date of his hiring. This was followed by detailed descriptions of the contributions he had made since. Thanks to the careful analysis of his functions, this list showed a steady increase of responsibilities, up to and including the responsibilities normally assumed by a Division Administrator. It made a fine record of accomplishment—an onward and upward report that stood out in sharp contrast to a job title and salary that showed no change whatever. Then he headed the report with a title page which read:

"To Mrs. George Wiley from George Wiley.

"Subject: Financial and progress forecast for the next twelve months, with alternatives for improvement, on the occasion of our tenth wedding anniversary."

(Experience has proven that the use of anniversary dates is one of the most disarming techniques in getting around "lines of command." Almost any anniversary can be used—the birthday of a key executive; the date you joined the company, the company's "founder's day," or date of incorporation; the birth of a child and the subsequent passing out of cigars, and similar occasions.)

Under favorable circumstances, George could have taken his "anniversary promise to his wife" to his boss with a smiling suggestion that he check it for accuracy. That step being out of the question, George put in a phone call to the key executive who had had the final word on hiring him.

When that dignitary answered, George said, "My wife and I had a long talk last night about my work here. You came into the picture because you were the one who hired me and assigned me to my job. You gave me such an inspiring talk that day that I wish there was some way I could talk things over with you again."

"Nothing easier," replied the executive. "I see I've got a luncheon open next week. Make it then."

George handed over the report, without comment, as the table was being cleared, and before the coffee was served. The executive read it unsmilingly, and handed it back.

"What do you want me to do about it?" he asked.

"I don't know that you can do anything," said George. "I don't seem to have any alternative but to leave, much as I like the company as a whole. What I really want is your advice."

Between being flattered by the request for his advice, and challenged by a situation about which he might be helpless, the executive said, "Let me borrow that report of yours for a few days. I'm getting a couple of ideas I can't talk about now, but I'll call you Monday if not sooner. My only advice right now is not to do anything until you hear from me."

And on Monday George began a series of interviews within the company that brought him a $2,200 raise.

In this case the four-point formula was modified only enough to get around a recalcitrant boss. George knew he had earned a raise. His boss knew it but refused to do anything about it. So George resorted to diplomacy to let a higher executive know he had earned a raise. And he made sure, through the presentation of his "forecast," that this top executive knew that George knew that he had earned his raise.

Every man and woman has different experiences and faces different situations in getting a raise, but the case history of Wiley will serve as a flexible guide. The general principle of filling out the aforementioned forms is to compel yourself to "think on paper." Such "written thinking" will do much to clarify your position and reveal why you are uniquely deserving of a raise even though the "annual review" might be months in the future. In their final drafts, the four forms should reveal that you have self-confidence, without arrogance or egotism. They should indicate a knowledge of your own worthwhileness, a belief in your value to the company, and a genuine concern in doing whatever may be necessary to continue your—and the company's progress.

Raises versus Promotions

A popular misconception is that raises and promotions are the same thing, and it is usually true that a promotion and a raise go hand in hand. But raises are far less often accompanied by promotions. A good worker gets his raise when he does the same job better as a result of increased skill and experience. The senior stenographer in the office stenographic pool makes more than the newcomer, but technically she is still a stenographer. A stone cutter with the skill and experience to carve elaborate friezes for modern buildings may command a tremendous salary, but he is still a stone cutter, and will remain so, low on the status totem pole, unless he wants to open his own shop and become a sculptor—an enormous increase in status too often accompanied by a drop in income.

A promotion is an advancement to a position with a title and responsibilities that indicate a change for the better in your prestige and power. It may be accompanied by a substantial raise, or admit you to the company profit-sharing plan, or provide an extra week's vacation, or do no more than give you a key to the executive's men's room. But unless you are "kicked upstairs" to a pretentious but empty title, as some companies do when they can't retire aging executives soon enough, a promotion is a recognition of your ability to assume responsibility for the work of others as well as yourself.

The mere fact that others are involved alters considerably your approach to your work. Whereas before you were concerned with how well you did your job, and what the boss thought about your work, you are now concerned about how well you and your subordinates do the job, what you think about them, what they think about you, and above all, what your superiors think about you in particular and your department in general.

All of which brings up the subject of company politics. The man with his nose to the grindstone can remain aloof from company politics because neither he nor his obdurate nose are going anywhere anyway. But you are concerned with your subordinates and your superiors, and where you are concerned with people, you are concerned with politics. In that spot there are no neutrals—only insiders and outsiders, and you can't help steer the ship unless you are a recognized member of the crew.

If you want to continue to be prompted up the managerial ladder, you must realize that the higher you go, the smarter will be the men with whom you must play politics. In his famous best-selling book, *The Status Seekers*, Author Vance Packard asserts that it is becoming increasingly difficult for non-college graduates to win top managerial positions, the implication being that college men can get along together more smoothly than their rougher contemporaries who came up "the hard way."

My own experience with both college and non-college men in approximately equal numbers gives the college men the advantage in only one easily remedied respect. The college man is trained to "think rich," and moves confidently ahead on the assurance that his diploma will carry him through. No matter that he may be poverty-stricken in the ability department; he is rich in college associates and rich in thought. What he can't do himself, his air of confidence often will help him do. Confronted with this collegiate self-assurance, the non-college man tends to go on the defensive, and few are the sales made when the pitch is in defense of the product instead of in the assertion of its merits.

Two things must be taken into consideration here. Success is an accumulative thing. The higher you go, the more responsibilities you accumulate. To the vast majority, college or non-college, this accumulation of responsibilities and the resulting "high pressure" becomes a terrifying thing, and they tend to slack off just when the going is good. At the same time, the higher you go, the more experience you have in handling responsibilities, and the more subordinates you have to handle them. And if you haven't left the selection of your subordinates to intelligence tests and letters of recommendation from "old grads," you've got a loyal crew behind you shoving you ahead for their own good.

If what I say next sounds derogatory to college educations, it is not because I am not in favor of colleges.

I am in favor of all the education a man can get. What I do object to is the smug assumption that what a man learns in four years of ivy-walled seclusion, during which he may or may not have achieved anything worth mentioning, is going to last him the rest of his life. As the old Latin proverb has it, "A good man is always a good learner," one of the few proverbs as good today as then. The reverse of that, equally true, is that a good learner is always a good man, only in that case college has nothing to do with it.

As I have pointed out, the habit of success is based on a constant study of your achievements and their relation to how you want to function in life. This is no ivory-towered study to be completed in four years and then forgotten. It is an unending and ever-expanding process through which you accumulate increasingly valuable experiences. And when these achievements are written down and analyzed in terms of value to your organization and yourself, you will have living dollar signs speaking for you with far more authority than can a dusty diploma.

Finding the Line of Power

At 31, Walter Basel was a sales engineer doing most of the field work for the Department Sales Manager. Because he was seldom in the home office, he had few opportunities to participate in office politics, and because of that, too, he was usually "out of sight—out of mind" when choice assignments came up. His Functional Self-Analysis supported his ambition to become an inside executive, but how to get that idea across to his superiors when they hardly knew him by sight?

To emphasize his difficulty, Basel brought in an organization chart of the company which clearly revealed the responsibilities of every man from floor washer to president, and just who reported to whom, and for what.

"You see, my boss is sitting on top of the whole sales department," he explained. "There is no one else I can go to without crossing organization lines, and I'd get my ears pinned back if I did that."

It was a beautiful chart, almost as complicated as the genealogical chart of Queen Elizabeth, but I was unimpressed. "This is the way the company wishes it was," I said. "A place for each man, and every man in his place, like tools in an efficient tool room. But men aren't as easily placed as tools, and that's what makes an organization chart a pretty dead thing. It shows the line of command, but it doesn't show the line of power."

"Double-talk," said Basel.

"Not at all. Some of these executives carry their own weight in their departments, but others ride on the title while another man, usually more quiet and approachable, has most of the responsibility. You have heard something like, 'It's all right to put the requisition through channels, but if you really want action, tell Hank.' Well, Hank might not be listed on the line of command, but when it comes to getting something done, he's on the line of power. And you can reach Hank without crossing organization lines."

Basel found his "Hank" in the person of the mild-mannered man who served as secretary to the Executive Vice President. To all intents and purposes, he had no more to say about what went on in the company than did the pencil with which he took notes, but what the V.P. didn't know about the company, he did.

Basel made his first approach by borrowing a technical manual from the front office, "to bone up for his field trip." When he returned from his trip he returned the book with a note: "The company I called on is using the procedures described on Page 17, but with some modifications I think you should know about. Looked good to me. I think Mr. K. (the head of another department) would be interested."

As Basel expected, he was called in to elaborate on his note, but when the secretary suggested he pass the information along to Mr. K. in person, he pleaded organization lines. "I don't want the word getting back to my boss that I've been going over his head."

"I get it," approved the secretary. "Just a minute, and I'll clear it with the head man." Two minutes later Basel was in the V.P.'s office explaining the modifications he had encountered.

"I'll be glad to write up a full report," he volunteered.

"Okay, write it up," said the V.P.

In reporting the conversation to me, Basel was emotionally upset. "It was a run-around. The head man didn't smile. He showed no interest or enthusiasm. I know he just told me to write up the report to get rid of me."

It took a little explaining, but finally Basel appreciated the fact that the V.P. had been shown nothing to get enthusiastic about. All talk, possibly constructive talk, but still nothing had actually happened.

"You got what you wanted," I said. "The head man paid some attention to you, which was more than you expected, and now your Mr. K. will be showing you some attention if you write up the kind of a report he can use. Now you've got to really get to work to make that report good."

During the next four months Basel made two more long field trips, borrowed six books from the secretary, and turned in two more constructive reports. The secretary knew what Basel was up to, and so did the V.P., but they appreciated his extra efforts, especially when one report led to an unexpected sale. Under those circumstances, executives will usually cooperate with the man who is making his program effective; in fact, I have hundreds of cases to prove that they will clear a path for him. They did for Basel when they made him Mr. K.'s assistant at a substantial increase in salary, and took him off the road at a substantial increase in domestic bliss.

Tradition has it that Opportunity knocks but once. How typical of tradition—waiting for something as attractive as Opportunity to come around seeking you. How much more gallant to go out seeking her, especially now that she is no longer hard to find if you know where to look. The techniques described in this chapter can be adjusted to lead you there from no matter whence you might start.

chapter **12**

SUCCESS IS YOUR BIRTHRIGHT

Life and Progress Are Inseparable

Every historical fact confirms the creativeness of man and glorifies his efforts to improve himself, often against pathetic odds. Both in the Old and New Testaments are many references to the joys of work. Socrates said, "He is idle who might be better employed." Lowell said, "No man is born into the world whose work is not born with him." And by way of bringing these and countless supporting sayings up to date, Dale Carnegie said, "If you don't find happiness in your work, you may never find it anywhere."

At the same time, Myron Clark, past president of the Society for the Advancement of Management had to report more recently, "More than eighty per cent of our working people are in jobs which do not use their best abilities, and which, therefore, do not provide the satisfactions associated with success."

The appalling feature of Mr. Clark's statement is that

it caused few raised eyebrows. That 80 per cent of our people should be functioning on their lesser abilities has been true for so many centuries that it is taken for granted, and what is taken for granted is seldom a cause for action. Yet as I pointed out earlier, the man in a job that uses his lesser abilities has to strain himself to the utmost to turn out a mediocre performance, while the man using his best abilities sails through his work with built-in efficiency and satisfaction.

Some day in the not too distant future, the tremendous increase in productivity that can be ours when 80 per cent of the people are using their best abilities will become apparent to all. Then a veritable Manhattan Project of scientists, economists, humanists and industrialists will be turned loose to discover how to release this greatest source of power ever put on earth. A power for peace, production, and universal happiness.

You're on Your Own

In the meantime, it is still each man largely for himself, and to the man who knows what his best abilities are, and uses them, goes the success. This is true regardless of his age, religion, color, education, or current position on the status totem pole. And that is why this book details the procedures by which a man can come to know his best abilities, his Dynamic Success Factors, and use them to make a habit of success.

I believe that in order to feel alive, a man must feel that he is growing, that he is continuously becoming more useful. The alternative—working day after day and year after year at routine tasks merely to keep his physical husk alive—is a form of occupational vegetating that dulls both the mind and the spirit. That kind of work is penal servitude for ambition, and when ambition sees itself sentenced to serve 20 or more years of drudgery before achieving the success of Social Security, it just curls up and quits.

Yet most people trapped in jobs unworthy of their

talents claim that security is their goal, and that in attaining a secure job they have achieved success. Don't ever believe it. In today's changing times, jobs that have been "secure" for decades may be declared obsolete tomorrow. Government bureaus are swept by economy waves or "streamlined for greater efficiency"; a newly-elected mayor may be the new broom that makes a clean sweep through the old-timers at city hall; old line companies merge with new companies and whole departments are abolished; and always, of course, there is the chance that the vagaries of health may demand a change of climate. Occupational security exists only when confidence in one's known abilities exists.

Probably the most insidious result of "secure" work is the wilting effect that it has on your best abilities. At first a man may feel frustrated at not using his best abilities, but as time passes, and he "gets used to the work," he eases his frustrations by "making the best of it." In this form of rationalization, he elevates the minor abilities he uses on the job to the status of his best abilities, and his unused best abilities simply wither away from neglect. When this process continues over a period of years, the unfortunate man has so mentally soothed his frustrations that he no longer wants to use his best abilities because he has "forgotten" he has them.

To some extent this withering effect takes place even on a job that may use two or three of your Dynamic Success Factors. Those that are unused lie dormant. But they don't die. When you seek them out through an analysis of your achievements, and revive them with attention they will flourish to make you the complete person you want to be. And in the process you may discover some success factors so long dormant that you didn't know you had them.

It is only through being your best self that you can live up to your potentialities. When every morning you can face the day filled with expectation instead of resignation, you are well on the way to performing at your best. The added factor is that what is best for you is best for the others around you. The successful man is not he who gets ahead by climbing over others, but he who gets ahead by producing the values that are of service to others.

Don't Knock Your Competitor

Remember that you will not be the only one who is producing services of value. Whenever a choice job opens up, you can count on facing some stiff competition in your efforts to land it. In many cases the rivalry can be a bitter, dog-eat-dog affair in which more reputations are destroyed than built. No one profits from such a struggle. In that respect I am reminded of the executive who had three men struggling fiercely for a top spot. "I had to hire a man from outside," he told me. "If I had promoted one of the three, the other two would have quit rather than work for him. Then I would have had to hire three new credit men instead of one new credit manager."

Competitors are really cooperators. You can be sure that if no one else wants the job, it is not apt to be much good. When the rivalry is keen, you are inspired to try with the best that's in you, and if that is not enough, you are inspired to strengthen what you've got for a better try next time. If no one is competing with you, if you never have to dig to find the best that's in you, you may never know just how good your best might be. Never worry about the competition. Worry produces fear and hate, and fear and hate can take up so much room in your mind and so color your thinking that you can't present your best side at all.

Raymond Carmody's case presents a typical example. He was one of three regional sales managers being considered to replace the retiring national sales manager. He was doing everything possible to prepare himself for the job, including coming to me for counsel. I could agree with that line of reasoning, but Carmody hadn't talked to me five minutes before I could see that he was more worried about what the manager of the western division would do than what he could do himself. I think he expected me to produce some trick to circumvent his rival.

After he had completed the procedures described in this book, his confidence in himself was foremost in his mind, but his resentment of Henderson, the western division man, had in no way diminished.

"All right," I said. "You have analyzed the functions of the national sales manager's job, and you have agreed that the most important function is to build and lead the best sales team possible. Where does Henderson fit into this team?"

"I don't care where he fits in," said Carmody, his resentment flaring up. "He can quit if he wants to, and I hope he does."

"Yet you say he is an excellent salesman. Is he better than you?"

Carmody calmed down, and after a moment he gave me an honest answer. "No, though his sales top mine for some months. On a year-round average, however, my sales are ahead of his."

"In that case," I said, "I don't think you should get the national sales manager's job."

Carmody looked at me as though he had been betrayed, but before he could release his rage I said, "Any national sales manager who doesn't care whether a top regional manager quits or not isn't very interested in his team."

A long silence, and the rage Carmody had built up faded away. "I get it," he said. "He's a good man, and I'll need him if I get the job. Now what do I do?"

We helped him develop a sales management program which could lead to a more effective use of Henderson and the other members of the team. When the three rivals were called in by the president, one at a time, to present their qualifications for the job, Carmody was the only one with a written program that included a plan for the continued cooperation of the team.

He got the job. Furthermore, having stressed Henderson's excellent sales record in his program, he won that salesman around to his side, albeit not overnight. But by sending memoranda of appreciation every time Henderson completed a good sale—with a carbon copy to the president—he turned the once bitter rivalry into lasting friendship, proving once again that if you want others to see good in you, first see the good in others, and let them know you see it.

The Chinese have a proverb that reads: "A bit of fragrance clings to the hand that gives flowers." This also goes for the verbal or written bouquet. Say something nice to someone, and a bit of its niceness will cling to you. We say that you can't get something for nothing in this life, as negative a statement as ever was made. The positive side of it, equally true, is that you can't *give* something for nothing. The man who finds good things to say about others will find others saying good things about him. And while one man saying a good thing to another is only one man expressing an opinion, when a lot of men begin saying good things about one man, you've got a consensus.

Alvin Dorset discovered the truth of the above paragraph by what he called at first a "revolting experiment." He had an excellent job with an excellent company, but as he explained it, "There's one guy in that office I just can't stomach, I don't know what there is about him, but just having him seated two desks away is enough to ruin my day. He's become such an obsession with me that either I quit or I'm going to slug him one of these days and get fired. At least that way I'll get severance pay."

Alvin completed the procedures described in this book before I returned again to the object of his personal animus. Then I said, "Mr. Dorset, I know you did a lot of soul-searching when you began listing your achievements and analyzing them. But you did locate your Dynamic Success Factors, and you know they are being used effectively in your present job. Now this chap seated two desks away—don't you suppose there must be something good about him that enables him to function well enough to hold a job in your line of work?"

"What do you want me to do?" asked Dorset bitterly,

"analyze his achievements and make him successful? Why, I'd—"

"Not at all," I interrupted quickly. "But you told me that you didn't know what there was about him that you didn't like. I suggest you find out, remembering, of course, to look for the good points that count, and not the weak. Oh, I know that in football they say to hunt for the weak points in the line, and run the plays through there, but you can be sure that the coach who uses that strategy has spent many a nervous hour analyzing all the strong points first. He knows his opponent isn't winning games by featuring weak points in the line, and your friend isn't holding down a good job with weaknesses and mistakes. If he didn't have any good points there, he wouldn't be there, either."

"How revolting can you get?" said Dorset. But the idea of seeking some good points in his hated office-mate intrigued him. He became more intrigued when he discovered a couple of points that made his associate look almost human. These are the points that are always invisible when you are looking only for the bad, just as success becomes almost invisible when you study only mistakes. To find more good points, Dorset struck up a coffee-break conversation with his associate that was resumed the next day. After a week of this the associate said, "Dorset, I had you pegged for one of those 'look-down-the-nosers' that I can't stand. But you seem to be a right guy."

"Now that you describe it," said Dorset, "I guess that was my opinion of you."

Two weeks later, Dorset and his new friend began collaboration on a new car-unloading and materials-handling program for the company that is already saving thousands of dollars a year. And I'll always like Dorset's somewhat dazed comment to me: "So help me," he said, "I didn't get his raise for him. He got mine for me."

This is not "do-gooder" advice that I am thrusting at you. It is cold, practical business advice. When you speak well of and to your associates, they will think and speak well of you, and when there are a dozen men to say,

"Well, if anyone deserves a promotion, Hank does," no supervisor has to hesitate in putting the promotion through even though the "annual review" be months in the future.

Good words make good friends; ill words make enemies. No words, meaning staying out of company politics to keep the nose to the grindstone, means no words in return, including such highly prized words as "raise" and "promotion." Look for what's good in others, and they'll look for what's good in you.

In analyzing your achievements, you learned how to seek out and evaluate the best that's in you so you can bring the best that's in you out. You can apply the same process in discovering the best that is in your fellow-workers, and in letting them know that you know they are good. Here you face the challenge of having one or two be so inspired by your constructive words that they will beat you to your promotion. Good! As I mentioned earlier, a keen competitor is your best collaborator in compelling you to seek out every talent you've got, and use it for all it's worth. That's living.

I want to carry that thought one step further. As I have mentioned earlier, the successful man is not the one who climbs over others but who is of most service to others. The higher you go, the more people you can serve, and to be practical about it, the more people you will have serving you. Discouraging, isn't it, to realize that if they are the average employees Myron Clark spoke about, 80 per cent of them are not giving you their best abilities? Your own success is being slowed down by the inertia of employees who are living to punch the time clock on the way home to freedom.

This will not be the case if you have made a habit of recognizing the best that's in you, and the best that's in your associates. The best employer is the man with the best employees, and he doesn't get them until he learns how to recognize and appreciate a good employee when he has one. This invaluable education starts when you begin to look for the best qualities in your associates. Then when you get your promotion, you will be able to use their best qualities in support of your own, and the executive with that kind of support has at least twice the strength of the executive who stands alone.

Top management is gradually becoming aware of this fact. Recently the president of DuPont said, "Each individual should be given the opportunity to exploit his talents to the fullest, in the way best suited to his personality. The uncommon man may be far more valuable than the man who is obsessed with keeping his nose clean." Supporting this statement is one from Chairman C. F. Craig of A.T.&T. "If we want the exceptional qualities of men to emerge to the full, we must remove all limitations to growth. We must encourage each man to grow in his own way." To that I will add that if a supervisor is not able to recognize the best talents in his men, and find room for the development of those talents, he is no supervisor.

The day when each man's abilities will be recognized, and he will be guided to his success through his talents instead of being left to "make a living" by the sweat of his brow is fast approaching, but unless you want to wait for it, each man is still—and excitingly—in command of his own success. It is still up to you, but hard-headed, practical counsellor though I must be, I must also admit that no man can stand alone. You need God.

I'm not going to go religious on you. All I'm going to say is that God is the source of power, and you need all the power you can get. It would be presumptious of me, a layman, to tell you how to reach this source of power when the house of your own faith is just around the corner. Visit it. And read some of the inspiring books on the power of faith. If you don't know where to start, I would suggest any of the works of Dr. Norman Vincent Peale to put you on the right track. In revealing the power of God, Dr. Peale also reveals the power God gave man to work and achieve for His greater glory. That power is yours for the asking, anywhere, any time, any place. No long distance toll charges and never a busy signal when you call on God.

My layman's sermon ends with this quote from a Detroit industrialist: "Time is my biggest problem. What with planning committees, sales meetings, directors' conferences, and advertising campaigns—not to mention what I go through in figuring out corporation taxes and the annual budget—I have to make every minute pay. So you wonder where I find the time for my work with the Business Men's Christian League on Wednesday night, and my work as deacon and usher of my church on Sunday? That's where I get the strength to make the rest of my work pay. Believe me, your work for God not only pays, but it puts the pay in the work you do professionally."

The Art of Changing Careers

A few pages back I listed a few of the reasons why "job security" is a myth that must be replaced by the reality of "ability security." But the very reasons that make jobs insecure—obsolescence, automation, decentralization, company mergers and the like—are in themselves symptoms of progress and greater productivity, and hence more security. I'll admit that the senior bookkeeper who found himself reduced to bill collector when his job was absorbed by electronic calculating machines thought he had been sabotaged by progress, but now that he has found his real abilities and is using them as a tax consultant, his proudest possession is a new electronic calculator.

Changes like that can vary between painful and disastrous for the man who is unprepared for them, while the man who is prepared welcomes them for the opportunities they provide. And the changes will be coming faster. According to figures from the Department of Labor, new types of jobs are being created at a rate of better than two per cent a year. Project that progress report ahead six years, and it means that one out of seven of us will be employed in a job category that doesn't exist at the present.

Following that same "rate of change" projection, each year I advise my senior students at Fairleigh Dickinson

University that fully one-third of them have prepared themselves for careers that will be outmoded within a generation. Invariably this statement is greeted with groans accompanied by such bitter cracks as, "How can you study for a career if it's not going to be there?"

My answer to that is, "You aren't selling the label put on a chosen career, but the intelligence and talents of the man who chooses it. Your career label can change, but there will always be a demand for your abilities. The only real shortage in this world is in the number of people who know how to use their best abilities for the advancement of themselves and others."

Then I add, "When you prepare yourself for progress, you are preparing to double your earning power while doubling your hours of leisure. When you prepare yourself for a label, such as a title on the door, you are saying you want to leave things as they are. Now which do you really want—all the fantastic wonders of the future, or the world pretty much in the condition your fathers have it now?"

To that question they can return only one answer. Let's go! And since that can be the only answer, let's see what that means to you and your success. During the next ten years there will continue to be a serious shortage of men of management caliber. This is due to the relatively low birthrate during the depression years of the Thirties plus the frightful loss of our choicest young men during the war years. This means there will be a continued demand for older men of executive ability, and increasing pressure on the younger men and women to develop their executive abilities and earn their promotions as soon as possible.

Under these circumstances the opportunities have never been greater for men retiring at relatively young ages from military, government, and municipal positions. As of now, to the great loss of industry, most of these highly qualified persons have failed to take advantage of these opportunities because they have failed to relate a lifetime of military or civil service experience with similar backgrounds in industry. From the thousands of case histories in my files, let me mention just briefly two examples. The first concerns a naval architect who had spent 30 years at his profession in the Navy, rising to the rank of Captain. But as he told me, "I'm an expert on armor plating, and the need for that is about as obsolete as I am. The only offer I could get was five thousand a year in a small boat yard because they thought my rank would carry weight when I had to dish out orders."

He saw an entirely different picture by the time he had completed Functional Self-Analysis. Though he had enjoyed his work as a naval architect, specializing in armor-plating installations running into millions of dollars, the achievement in which he had found his greatest satisfaction had been in clearing a harbor of sunken ships, and installing new port facilities. Today, as the executive vice-president of a harbor-dredging and dock-building firm at $25,000 a year, he says, "I am a younger man today than when I was commissioned as an ensign in the Navy."

The second case history concerns a retired Colonel who found through Success Factor Analysis that he was a fully qualified city administrator. For 25 of his 30 years in the Army he had been either training or leading combat troops, but for what he called "five glorious years" he had been an occupation officer in charge of restoring one war-ravaged city after another. His greatest success had been achieved through working with local city officials, not all of whom had reason to love the Yanks whose shells had driven out the Germans to the great detriment of personal and public property.

Today he is the city manager of a town of 40,000, and though the town has switched its political allegiance from Democrat to Republican and back again, no one has ever suggested a switch in city managers. He is one happy man. And when you consider the hundreds of types of managerial jobs that are open and begging for occupants, and when you consider that you need but "functionalize" your past achievements in terms of these open opportunities to make them attainable, you may discover the full significance of the quotation from Lowell stated earlier: "No man is born into the world whose work is not born with him." The entire career to which you thought you had devoted your professional life may have been merely a preparation of your talents for this new job you were really born to do.

To the young men just starting out to meet a future filled with change, I would like to sound, of all things, a note of caution. When technical changes come to an industry, as when transistors and diodes nearly wiped out the booming electronic tube industry, whole companies are affected. During the next few years you will see multi-million dollar companies changing careers with the flexibility of individuals, and even in the big old-line companies, old products will be dropped and new ones added with bewildering rapidity. The paint company you worked for today may be a plastics firm tomorrow, and the plastics firm may find itself in the automobile business a few weeks later, molding car bodies. At the same time, diversification will be the order of the day. The company with five major products on the market can survive the overnight obsolescence of one as long as it has four to carry it while it is reaching for two more.

All of this means that companies faced with changing products and changing careers are also faced with changing attitudes and changing philosophies. Only a few years ago a firm described as a "staid old business house" was a bulwark of security. Today, unless it has changed its attitude and philosophy, it is on the way out. Thus the young man entering this challenging world of tomorrow must bring with him a new understanding of things as they will be. Your father could groom himself to be the head of a department and achieve his goal; today you have no assurance that either you or the department will be there.

Don't groom yourself to become the head of a department. Groom yourself to be a department head, and you can let the changes come as they may. This same rule applies to all jobs in government, commerce, and industry. Job labels and career labels are going to change, but when you know what your talents are, and where they can function to best advantage, you don't have to worry about labels. It's the product inside—the best that's in you—that you have to sell, and you can write your own label.

Write a good one. Executives heading new departments, developing new products, are like impulse buyers in a new super-market—they can't be sure of what they want, but they are eager to give a tempting package a try.

A Word to the Ladies

During the next ten years the demand for women in management will increase at three times the rate for men. At the same time there will be a substantial increase in the demand for women in all forms of service activities, from international diplomacy to community youth training programs. Our increasing leisure, too, will have the effect of providing more work for women as travel agents, recreational supervisors, airplane and ship hostesses, resort manageresses, national park guides and allied occupations.

An urgent word to women who may have special talents in the fields of teaching, nursing, and religious works. I am only saying what has already been said when I say the need for you is already desperate, but I want to add my own plea. You may not think you are qualified to work in these areas, but please take a second look at your achievements in the light of what you have read.

Listen to what one school superintendent told me. "I've got ten teachers on my staff that I pirated from another school that is worse off than we are. Five of my senior teachers are working double sessions to make up for the teachers I still lack. Yet I know there are at least fifty women in this town who have all it takes to be excellent teachers if only they realized it. I'm not saying they'll get rich, but we're not paying peanuts, either. How do you wake them up?"

Well, you don't. I can't wake you up. The superintendent can't wake you up. But you can awaken yourself. You may have all it takes already, or you may need only a refresher course in night or summer school to make good in the job you were born to do. The same applies to nursing, religious work, and community service. Please, won't you analyze your success factors, and see if your best job might not still lie ahead?

What Is This Thing—The Best That's In You?

In answer to the question above, I hope you never find out. When you have made a habit of success, the best that is in you will be still in the process of development when you make at some venerable age that final try. Recently I attended an award dinner for a retiring executive, in the course of which he received the traditional gold watch and the following accolade from the president: "Mr. Johanns, known to all of us as Joe, has served this company for forty years, and has left an enviable record all of us can shoot at. From his start as a sander in the finishing department to his present position as vice president in charge of production, he has never been satisfied with doing an average job. It had to be better-than-average, or he didn't want his name connected with it."

The voice droned on, but I had heard all I wanted to hear. It was all there in those words—"better-than-average." They explained why a vice-president of 65 was being handed his gold watch by a president of 47. In terms of achievement, doing an average job means you are holding your own. It follows, then, that to get ahead, you must do better than average, which is not necessarily very much. That happens to be a loaded statement.

In any business, average performance is a known quality. It is calculated in production units and plotted on graphs, and may well be the backbone of the theory called "Management by Exception." Anyone with the power of observation has but to look around him to see what the average performance of his fellow-workers amounts to, and nudge his own performance a notch above. In so doing, he is dealing with the known. So well known, in fact, that it can be plotted on a graph.

But the best that is in you goes far beyond anything that can be plotted on a chart. When you have analyzed your achievements and discovered through Success Factor Analysis the areas in which success becomes your domain, you are only at last beginning to appreciate what you can really do. I wish I had you in front of me, so I could pound on the desk if necessary, to deliver this final truth:

For the man who doesn't know his real abilities, and therefore turns in the average performance, the chart is drawn.

For the man who recognizes the average performance of his fellows, and sets his course a notch above, the way is more remunerative but still confined to paralleling the known average.

But for the man who knows his own abilities and uses them, there is no ceiling. He is not content with the average performance of others. For him "above average performance" is not the course, nor even the start of it.

Success is his goal, and each success achieved leads on to greater ones. And thus in making a habit of success, he will find that success has made a habit of him. That's all.

In establishing this habit, may you find it incurable.

Index

218

222

G

H

224

225

236

THE BEST OF THE BESTSELLERS
FROM WARNER BOOKS!

THE BEST OF THE BESTSELLERS
FROM WARNER BOOKS!

THE KINGDOM by Ronald Joseph   **(81-467, $2.50)**
The saga of a passionate and powerful family who carves out of the
wilderness the largest cattle ranch in the world. Filled with both
adventure and romance, hard-bitten empire building and tender
moments of intimate love, **The Kingdom** is a book for all readers.

BLUE SKIES, NO CANDY by Gael Greene   **(81-368, $2.50)**
"How in the world were they able to print **Blue Skies, No Candy**
without some special paper that resists **Fahrenheit 451?** (That's the
burning point of paper!) This sizzling sexual odyssey elevates Ms.
Greene from her place at the head of the food-writing list into the
Erica Jong pantheon of sexually liberated fictionalists."—Liz Smith,
New York Daily News

THESE GOLDEN PLEASURES   **(82-416, $2.25)**
by Valerie Sherwood
From the stately mansions of the east to the freezing hell of the
Klondike, beautiful Roxanne Rossiter went after what she wanted
—and got it all! By the author of the phenomenally successful
This Loving Torment.

THE OTHER SIDE OF THE MOUNTAIN:
PART 2 by E.G. Valens   **(82-463, $2.25)**
Part 2 of the inspirational story of a young Olympic contender's
courageous climb from paralysis and total helplessness to a useful
life and meaningful marriage. An NBC-TV movie and serialized in
Family Circle magazine.

 A Warner Communications Company

Please send me the books I have checked.

Enclose check or money order only, no cash please. Plus 50¢ per
copy to cover postage and handling. N.Y. State residents add
applicable sales tax.

Please allow 2 weeks for delivery.

WARNER BOOKS
P.O. Box 690
New York, N.Y. 10019

Name ....
Address ....
City .... State .... Zip ....
_____ Please send me your free mail order catalog

IN 1942 THE U.S. RATIONED GASOLINE

The basic ration for passenger cars

A DRIVERS MUST DISPLAY THIS STICKER

That was wartime and the spirit of sacrifice was in the air. No one liked it, but everyone went along. Today we need a wartime spirit to solve our energy problems. A spirit of thrift in our use of all fuels, especially gasoline. We Americans pump over 200 million gallons of gasoline into our automobiles each day. That is nearly one-third the nation's total daily oil consumption and more than half of the oil we import every day . . . at a cost of some $40 billion a year. So conserving gasoline is more than a way to save money at the pump and help solve the nation's balance of payments, it also can tackle a major portion of the nation's energy problem. And that is something we all have a stake in doing . . . with the wartime spirit, but without the devastation of war or the inconvenience of rationing.

ENERGY CONSERVATION - IT'S YOUR CHANCE TO SAVE, AMERICA

Department of Energy, Washington, D.C.

A PUBLIC SERVICE MESSAGE FROM WARNER BOOKS, INC.